Michael j. Joens

From Zero to CEO: The Epic Journey of Building a Successful Business

Table of Contents: Introduction

Why start on the Journey of Building a Successful Business

Chapter 1:   5

Chapter 2:   32

Chapter 3   41

Chapter 4:   49

Chapter 5:   61

Chapter 6   66

Chapter 7   74

Chapter 8.   85

Chapter 9:   96

Chapter 10:   109

INTRODUCTION

Why you start on the Journey of Building a Successful Business

In the vast landscape of entrepreneurship, there are countless stories of individuals who have transformed their ideas into thriving businesses, defying the odds and redefining success. Behind every successful company lies an extraordinary journey, characterized by determination, innovation, and unwavering passion. This book chronicles the awe-inspiring path of building a business from scratch, capturing the highs, lows, and invaluable lessons learned along the way.

From the moment an ambitious entrepreneur conceives an idea, to the triumphant culmination of becoming a CEO, this book explores the intricacies and challenges faced in the process. Drawing upon the experiences of seasoned entrepreneurs, industry leaders, and innovative disruptors, we embark on an expedition into the realms of innovation, resourcefulness, and perseverance.

This captivating tale begins at ground zero, where visionaries dare to dream big and start small. We witness the initial spark of inspiration and the compelling drive to take action, often in the face of uncertainty and skepticism. Through captivating anecdotes and personal accounts, we unravel the strategies and mindsets that propelled these individuals from the depths of doubt to the heights of success.

As we delve into the various stages of entrepreneurship, we explore the art of transforming a raw idea into a tangible product or service. From market research and product development to branding and marketing, we unveil the secrets of identifying opportunities, crafting unique value propositions, and building a loyal customer base.

But building a successful business is not without its fair share of setbacks and obstacles. We delve into the challenges faced by entrepreneurs – the sleepless nights, financial pressures, and moments of self-doubt – and how they found the resilience to overcome them. Through tales of failure, we discover the invaluable lessons that pave the way for future triumphs.

Along this journey, we encounter the pivotal role of mentorship and networking, as entrepreneurs seek guidance from industry veterans and connect with like-minded individuals. We uncover the importance of creating a supportive community, where ideas are nurtured, collaborations are forged, and knowledge is shared, propelling entrepreneurs towards their ultimate vision.

Finally, we witness the transformation of these tenacious individuals into CEOs, as they navigate the complexities of scaling their businesses and leading teams. From building a company culture rooted in shared values and a growth mindset to making critical decisions in the face of uncertainty, we gain insight into the qualities that distinguish exceptional leaders.

Through the pages of this book, readers are invited to embark on an enlightening expedition, guided by the inspiring stories of entrepreneurs who turned dreams into reality. Whether you are an aspiring entrepreneur, a seasoned business owner, or simply a curious soul seeking inspiration, From Zero to CEO will ignite your entrepreneurial spirit and equip you with the knowledge and motivation to embark on your own epic journey of building a successful business.

Chapter 1:

Getting Started on the Road to Building a Successful Business

Starting a business is one of the most exciting and rewarding experiences you can have. But where do you begin? There are several ways to approach creating a business, with many important considerations. To help take the guesswork out of the process and improve your chances of success, follow our comprehensive guide on how to start a business. We'll walk you through each step of the process, from defining your business idea to registering, launching and growing your business

Before You Begin: Get in the Right Mindset
The public often hears about overnight successes because they make for a great headline. However, it's rarely that simple—they don't see the years of dreaming, building and positioning before a big public launch. For this reason, remember to focus on your business journey and don't measure your success against someone else's.

Consistency Is Key
New business owners tend to feed off their motivation initially but get frustrated when that motivation wanes. This is why it's essential to create habits and follow routines that power you through when motivation goes away.

Take the Next Step
Some business owners dive in headfirst without looking and make things up as they go along. Then, there are business owners who stay stuck in analysis paralysis and never start. Perhaps you're a mixture of the two—and that's right where you need to be. The best way to accomplish any business or personal goal is to write out every possible step it takes to achieve the goal. Then, order those steps by what needs to happen first. Some steps may take minutes while others take a long time. The point is to always take the next step.

1. Determine Your Business Concept

Most business advice tells you to monetize what you love, but it misses two other very important elements: it needs to be profitable and something you're good at. For example, you may love music, but how viable is your business idea if you're not a great singer or songwriter? Maybe you love making soap and want to open a soap shop in your small town that already has three close by—it won't be easy to corner the market when you're creating the same product as other nearby stores.

If you don't have a firm idea of what your business will entail, ask yourself the following questions:

•What do you love to do?

•What do you hate to do?

•Can you think of something that would make those things easier?

•What are you good at?

•What do others come to you for advice about?

•If you were given ten minutes to give a five-minute speech on any topic, what would it be?

•What's something you've always wanted to do, but lacked resources for?

These questions can lead you to an idea for your business. If you already have an idea, they might help you expand it. Once you have your idea, measure it against whether you're good at it and if it's profitable.

Your business idea also doesn't have to be the next Scrub Daddy or Squatty Potty. Instead, you can take an existing product and improve upon it. You can also sell a digital product so there's little overhead.

What Kind of Business Should You Start?

Before you choose the type of business to start, there are some key things to consider:

•What type of funding do you have?

•How much time do you have to invest in your business?

•Do you prefer to work from home or at an office or workshop?

•What interests and passions do you have?

•Can you sell information (such as a course), rather than a product?

•What skills or expertise do you have?

•How fast do you need to scale your business?

•What kind of support do you have to start your business?

•Are you partnering with someone else?

•Does the franchise model make more sense to you?

Consider Popular Business Ideas
Not sure what business to start? Consider one of these popular business ideas:
•Start a Franchise
•Start a Blog
•Start an Online Store
•Start a Dropshipping Business
•Start a Cleaning Business
•Start a Bookkeeping Business
•Start a Clothing Business
•Start a Landscaping Business
•Start a Consulting Business
•Start a Photography Business

•Start a Vending Machine Business

2. Research Your Competitors and Market

Most entrepreneurs spend more time on their products than they do getting to know the competition. If you ever apply for outside funding, the potential lender or partner wants to know: what sets you (or your business idea) apart? If market analysis indicates your product or service is saturated in your area, see if you can think of a different approach. Take housekeeping, for example—rather than general cleaning services, you might specialize in homes with pets or focus on garage cleanups.

Primary Research

The first stage of any competition study is primary research, which entails obtaining data directly from potential customers rather than basing your conclusions on past data. You can use questionnaires, surveys and interviews to learn what consumers want.

Surveying friends and family isn't recommended unless they're your target market. People who say they'd buy something and people who do are very different. The last thing you want is to take so much stock in what they say, create the product and flop when you try to sell it because all of the people who said they'd buy it don't because the product isn't something they'd actually buy.

Secondary Research

Utilize existing sources of information, such as census data, to gather information when you do secondary research. The current data may be studied, compiled and analyzed in various ways that are appropriate for your needs but it may not be as detailed as primary research.

Conduct a SWOT Analysis

SWOT stands for strengths, weaknesses, opportunities and threats. Conducting a SWOT analysis allows you to look at the facts about how your product or idea might perform if taken to market, and it can also help you make decisions about the direction of your idea. Your business idea might have some weaknesses that you hadn't considered or there may be some opportunities to improve on a competitor's product.

3. Create Your Business Plan

A business plan is a dynamic document that serves as a roadmap for establishing a new business. This document makes it simple for potential investors, financial institutions and company management to understand and absorb. Even if you intend to self-finance, a business plan can help you flesh out your idea and spot potential problems. When writing a well-rounded business plan, include the following sections:

Executive summary:
The executive summary should be the first item in the business plan, but it should be written last. It describes the proposed new business and highlights the goals of the company and the methods to achieve them.

Company description:
The company description covers what problems your product or service solves and why your business or idea is best. For example, maybe your background is in molecular engineering, and you've used that background to create a new type of athletic wear—you have the proper credentials to make the best material.

Market analysis:
This section of the business plan analyzes how well a company is positioned against its competitors. The market analysis should include target market, segmentation analysis, market size, growth rate, trends and a competitive environment assessment.

Organization and structure:

Write about the type of business organization you expect, what risk management strategies you propose and who will staff the management team. What are their qualifications? Will your business be a single-member limited liability company (LLC) or a corporation?

Mission and goals:
This section should contain a brief mission statement and detail what the business wishes to accomplish and the steps to get there. These goals should be SMART (specific, measurable, action-orientated, realistic and time-bound).

Products or services:
This section describes how your business will operate. It includes what products you'll offer to consumers at the beginning of the business, how they compare to existing competitors, how much your products cost, who will be responsible for creating the products, how you'll source materials and how much they cost to make.

Background summary:
This portion of the business plan is the most time-consuming to write. Compile and summarize any data, articles and research studies on trends that could positively and negatively affect your business or industry.

Marketing plan:
The marketing plan identifies the characteristics of your product or service, summarizes the SWOT analysis and analyzes competitors. It also discusses how you'll promote your business, how much money will be spent on marketing and how long the campaign is expected to last.

Financial plan:
The financial plan is perhaps the core of the business plan because, without money, the business will not move forward. Include a proposed budget in your financial plan along with projected financial statements, such as an income statement, a balance sheet and a statement of cash flows. Usually, five years of projected financial statements are acceptable. This section is also where you should include your funding request if you're looking for outside funding

Come Up With an Exit Strategy

An exit strategy is important for any business that is seeking funding because it outlines how you'll sell the company or transfer ownership if you decide to retire or move on to other projects. An exit strategy also allows you to get the most value out of your business when it's time to sell. There are a few different options for exiting a business, and the best option for you depends on your goals and circumstances.

The most common exit strategies are:
Selling the business to another party
Passing the business down to family members
Liquidating the business assets
Closing the doors and walking away
Develop a Scalable Business Model
As your small business grows, it's important to have a scalable business model so that you can accommodate additional customers without incurring additional costs. A scalable business model is one that can be replicated easily to serve more customers without a significant increase in expenses.

Some common scalable business models are:
•Subscription-based businesses
•Businesses that sell digital products
•Franchise businesses
•Network marketing businesses

Start Planning for Taxes

One of the most important things to do when starting a small business is to start planning for taxes. Taxes can be complex, and there are several different types of taxes you may be liable for, including income tax, self-employment tax, sales tax and property tax. Depending on the type of business you're operating, you may also be required to pay other taxes, such as payroll tax or unemployment tax.

4.Choose Your Business Structure

When structuring your business, it's essential to consider how each structure impacts the amount of taxes you owe, daily operations and whether your personal assets are at risk.

LLC

An LLC limits your personal liability for business debts. LLCs can be owned by one or more people or companies and must include a registered agent. These owners are referred to as members.

Pros

LLCs offer liability protection for the owners
They're one of the easiest business entities to set up
You can have a single-member LLC
Cons

You may be required to file additional paperwork with your state on a regular basis
LLCs can't issue stock
You'll need to pay annual filing fees to your state
Limited Liability Partnership (LLP)
An LLP is similar to an LLC but is typically used for licensed business professionals such as an attorney or accountant. These arrangements require a partnership agreement.

Pros

Partners have limited liability for the debts and actions of the LLP
LLPs are easy to form and don't require much paperwork
There's no limit to the number of partners in an LLP
Cons

Partners are required to actively take part in the business
LLPs can't issue stock
All partners are personally liable for any malpractice claims against the business
Sole Proprietorship

If you start a solo business, you might consider a sole proprietorship. The company and the owner, for legal and tax purposes, are considered the same. The business owner assumes liability for the business. So, if the business fails, the owner is personally and financially responsible for all business debts.

Pros

Sole proprietorships are easy to form
There's no need to file additional paperwork with your state
You're in complete control of the business
Cons

You're personally liable for all business debts
It can be difficult to raise money for a sole proprietorship
The business may have a limited lifespan
Corporation
A corporation limits your personal liability for business debts just as an LLC does. A corporation can be taxed as a C-corporation (C-corp) or an S-corporation (S-corp). S-corp status offers pass-through taxation to small corporations that meet certain IRS requirements. Larger companies and startups hoping to attract venture capital are usually taxed as C-corps.

Pros

Corporations offer liability protection for the owners
The life span of a corporation is not limited
A corporation can have an unlimited number of shareholders
Cons

Corporations are subject to double taxation
They're more expensive and complicated to set up than other business structures
The shareholders may have limited liability
Before you decide on a business structure, discuss your situation with a small business accountant and possibly an attorney, as each business type has different tax treatments that could affect your bottom line.

•Helpful Resources
•How To Set Up an LLC in 7 Steps
•How To Start a Sole Proprietorship
•How To Start a Corporation
•How To Start a Nonprofit
•How To Start a 501(c)(3)

5. Register Your Business and Get Licenses
There are several legal issues to address when starting a business after choosing the business structure. The following is a good checklist of items to consider when establishing your business:

Choose Your Business Name
Make it memorable but not too difficult. Choose the same domain name, if available, to establish your internet presence. A business name cannot be the same as another registered company in your state, nor can it infringe on another trademark or service mark that is already registered with the United States Patent and Trademark Office (USPTO).

Business Name vs. DBA

There are business names, and then there are fictitious business names known as "Doing Business As" or DBA. You may need to file a DBA if you're operating under a name that's different from the legal name of your business. For example, "Mike's Bike Shop" is doing business as "Mike's Bikes." The legal name of the business is "Mike's Bike Shop," and "Mike's Bikes" is the DBA.

You may need to file a DBA with your state, county or city government offices. The benefits of a DBA include:

It can help you open a business bank account under your business name
A DBA can be used as a "trade name" to brand your products or services
A DBA can be used to get a business license
Register Your Business and Obtain an EIN

You'll officially create a corporation, LLC or other business entity by filing forms with your state's business agency—usually the Secretary of State. As part of this process, you'll need to choose a registered agent to accept legal documents on behalf of your business. You'll also pay a filing fee. The state will send you a certificate that you can use to apply for licenses, a tax identification number (TIN) and business bank accounts.

Next, apply for an employer identification number (EIN). All businesses, other than sole proprietorships with no employees, must have a federal employer identification number. Submit your application to the IRS and you'll typically receive your number in minutes.

Get Appropriate Licenses and Permits
Legal requirements are determined by your industry and jurisdiction. Most businesses need a mixture of local, state and federal licenses to operate. Check with your local government office (and even an attorney) for licensing information tailored to your area.
•Helpful Resources
•Best LLC Services
•How To Register a Business Name
•How To Register a DBA
•How To Get an EIN for an LLC
•How To Get a Business License

6. Get Your Finances in Order
Open a Business Bank Account
Keep your business and personal finances separate. Here's how to choose a business checking account—and why separate business accounts are essential. When you open a business bank account, you'll need to provide your business name and your business tax identification number (EIN). This business bank account can be used for your business transactions, such as paying suppliers or invoicing customers. Most times, a bank will require a separate business bank account to issue a business loan or line of credit.

Hire a Bookkeeper or Get Accounting Software

If you sell a product, you need an inventory function in your accounting software to manage and track inventory. The software should have ledger and journal entries and the ability to generate financial statements.

Some software programs double as bookkeeping tools. These often include features such as check writing and managing receivables and payables. You can also use this software to track your income and expenses, generate invoices, run reports and calculate taxes.

There are many bookkeeping services available that can do all of this for you, and more. These services can be accessed online from any computer or mobile device and often include features such as bank reconciliation and invoicing. Check out the best accounting software for small business, or see if you want to handle the bookkeeping yourself.

Determine Your Break-Even Point
Before you fund your business, you must get an idea of your startup costs. To determine these, make a list of all the physical supplies you need, estimate the cost of any professional services you will require, determine the price of any licenses or permits required to operate and calculate the cost of office space or other real estate. Add in the costs of payroll and benefits, if applicable.

Businesses can take years to turn a profit, so it's better to overestimate the startup costs and have too much money than too little. Many experts recommend having enough cash on hand to cover six months of operating expenses.

When you know how much you need to get started with your business, you need to know the point at which your business makes money. This figure is your break-even point.

For example, let's say you're starting a small business that sells miniature birdhouses for fairy gardens. You have determined that it will cost you $500 in startup costs. Your variable costs are $0.40 per birdhouse produced, and you sell them for $1.50 each.

Let's write these out so it's easy to follow:

Fixed costs: $500 for the first month
Variable costs: 40 cents per birdhouse
Price per birdhouse: $1.50
The formula: $500/($1.50 - 40 cents)
$500 ÷ $1.10 = 456 units
This means that you need to sell at least 456 units just to cover your costs. If you can sell more than 456 units in your first month, you will make a profit.

7. Fund Your Business

There are many different ways to fund your business—some require considerable effort, while others are easier to obtain. Two categories of funding exist: internal and external.

Internal funding includes:

Personal savings
Credit cards
Funds from friends and family
If you finance the business with your own funds or with credit cards, you have to pay the debt on the credit cards and you've lost a chunk of your wealth if the business fails. By allowing your family members or friends to invest in your business, you are risking hard feelings and strained relationships if the company goes under. Business owners who want to minimize these risks may consider external funding.

External funding includes:

Small business loans
Small business grants
Angel investors
Venture capital
Crowdfunding

Small businesses may have to use a combination of several sources of capital. Consider how much money is needed, how long it will take before the company can repay it and how risk-tolerant you are. No matter which source you use, plan for profit. It's far better to take home six figures than make seven figures and only keep $80,000 of it.

Funding ideas include:

Invoice factoring: With invoice factoring, you can sell your unpaid invoices to a third party at a discount.

Business lines of credit: Apply for a business line of credit, which is similar to a personal line of credit. The credit limit and interest rate will be based on your business's revenue, credit score and financial history.

Equipment financing: If you need to purchase expensive equipment for your business, you can finance it with a loan or lease.

Small Business Administration (SBA) microloans: Microloans are up to $50,000 loans that can be used for working capital, inventory or supplies and machinery or equipment.

Grants: The federal government offers grants for businesses that promote innovation, export growth or are located in historically disadvantaged areas. You can also find grants through local and regional organizations.

Crowdfunding: With crowdfunding, you can raise money from a large group of people by soliciting donations or selling equity in your company.

Choose the right funding source for your business by considering the amount of money you need, the time frame for repayment and your tolerance for risk.

Helpful Resources
Best Small Business Loans
Best Startup Business Loans
Best Business Loans for Bad Credit
Business Loan Calculator
Average Business Loan Rates
How To Get a Business Loan.

8. Apply for Business Insurance

You need to have insurance for your business, even if it's a home-based business or you don't have any employees. The type of insurance you need depends on your business model and what risks you face. You might need more than one type of policy, and you might need additional coverage as your business grows. In most states, workers' compensation insurance is required by law if you have employees.

Work With an Agent To Get Insured

An insurance agent can help determine what coverages are appropriate for your business and find policies from insurers that offer the best rates. An independent insurance agent represents several different insurers, so they can shop around for the best rates and coverage options.

Basic Types of Business Insurance Coverage

•**Liability insurance** protects your business against third-party claims of bodily injury, property damage and personal injury such as defamation or false advertising.

•**Property insurance** covers the physical assets of your business, including your office space, equipment and inventory.

•**Business interruption insurance** pays for the loss of income if your business is forced to close temporarily due to a covered event such as a natural disaster.

•**Product liability insurance** protects against claims that your products caused bodily injury or property damage.

•**Employee practices liability insurance** covers claims from employees alleging discrimination, sexual harassment or other wrongful termination.

•**Workers' compensation insurance** covers medical expenses and income replacement for employees who are injured on the job.

Helpful Resources

•Best Small Business Insurance

•Best Commercial Auto Insurance

•How To Get Product Liability Insurance

•Your Guide to General Liability Insurance

•13 Types of Small Business Insurance.

9. Get the Right Business Tools

Business tools can help make your life easier and make your business run more smoothly. The right tools can help you save time, automate tasks and make better decisions.

Consider the following tools in your arsenal:

Accounting software: Track your business income and expenses, prepare financial statements and file taxes. Examples include QuickBooks and FreshBooks.

Customer relationship management (CRM) software: This will help you manage your customer relationships, track sales and marketing data and automate tasks like customer service and follow-ups. Examples include Zoho CRM and monday.com.

Project management software: Plan, execute and track projects. It can also be used to manage employee tasks and allocate resources. Examples include Airtable and ClickUp.

Credit card processor: This will allow you to accept credit card payments from customers. Examples include Stripe and PayPal.

Point of sale (POS): A system that allows you to process customer payments. Some accounting software and CRM software have POS features built-in. Examples include Clover and Lightspeed.

Virtual private network (VPN): Provides a secure, private connection between your computer and the internet. This is important for businesses that handle sensitive data. Examples include NordVPN and ExpressVPN.

Merchant services: When customers make a purchase, the money is deposited into your business account. You can also use merchant services to set up recurring billing or subscription payments. Examples include Square and Stripe.

Email hosting: This allows you to create a professional email address with your own domain name. Examples include G Suite and Microsoft Office 365.

10. Market Your Business

Many business owners spend so much money creating their products that there isn't a marketing budget by the time they've launched. Alternatively, they've spent so much time developing the product that marketing is an afterthought.

Create a Website

Even if you're a brick-and-mortar business, a web presence is essential. Creating a website doesn't take long, either—you can have one done in as little as a weekend. You can make a standard informational website or an e-commerce site where you sell products online. If you sell products or services offline, include a page on your site where customers can find your locations and hours. Other pages to add include an "About Us" page, product or service pages, frequently asked questions (FAQs), a blog and contact information.

Optimize Your Site for SEO

After getting a website or e-commerce store, focus on optimizing it for search engines (SEO). This way, when a potential customer searches for specific keywords for your products, the search engine can point them to your site. SEO is a long-term strategy, so don't expect a ton of traffic from search engines initially—even if you're using all the right keywords.

Create Relevant Content

Provide quality digital content on your site that makes it easy for customers to find the correct answers to their questions. Content marketing ideas include videos, customer testimonials, blog posts and demos. Consider content marketing one of the most critical tasks on your daily to-do list. This is used in conjunction with posting on social media.

Get Listed in Online Directories

Customers use online directories like Yelp, Google My Business and Facebook to find local businesses. Some city halls and chambers of commerce have business directories too. Include your business in as many relevant directories as possible. You can also create listings for your business on specific directories that focus on your industry.

Develop a Social Media Strategy
Your potential customers are using social media every day—you need to be there too. Post content that's interesting and relevant to your audience. Use social media to drive traffic back to your website where customers can learn more about what you do and buy your products or services.

You don't necessarily need to be on every social media platform available. However, you should have a presence on Facebook and Instagram because they offer e-commerce features that allow you to sell directly from your social media accounts. Both of these platforms have free ad training to help you market your business.

Helpful Resources
Best Website Builders
How To Make a Website for Your Business
The Best E-Commerce Platforms
Best Blogging Platforms
Best Web Hosting Services

11. Scale Your Business

To scale your business, you need to grow your customer base and revenue. This can be done by expanding your marketing efforts, improving your product or service, collaborating with other creators or adding new products or services that complement what you already offer.

Think about ways you can automate or outsource certain tasks so you can focus on scaling the business. For example, if social media marketing is taking up too much of your time, consider using a platform such as Hootsuite to help you manage your accounts more efficiently. You can also consider outsourcing the time-consumer completely.

You can also use technology to automate certain business processes, including accounting, email marketing and lead generation. Doing this will give you more time to focus on other aspects of your business.

When scaling your business, it's important to keep an eye on your finances and make sure you're still profitable. If you're not making enough money to cover your costs, you need to either reduce your expenses or find ways to increase your revenue.

Build a Team

As your business grows, you'll need to delegate tasks and put together a team of people who can help you run the day-to-day operations. This might include hiring additional staff, contractors or freelancers.

Resources for building a team include:

Hiring platforms: To find the right candidates, hiring platforms, such as Indeed and Glassdoor, can help you post job descriptions, screen résumés and conduct video interviews.

Job boards: Job boards such as Craigslist and Indeed allow you to post open positions for free.

Social media: You can also use social media platforms such as LinkedIn and Facebook to find potential employees.

Freelance platforms: Using Upwork, Freelancer and Fiverr can help you find talented freelancers for one-time or short-term projects. You can also outsource certain tasks, such as customer service, social media marketing or bookkeeping.

You might also consider partnering with other businesses in your industry. For example, if you're a wedding planner, you could partner with a florist, photographer, catering company or venue. This way, you can offer your customers a one-stop shop for all their wedding needs.

Another example is an e-commerce store that partners with a fulfillment center. This type of partnership can help you save money on shipping and storage costs, and it can also help you get your products to your customers faster.

To find potential partnerships, search for businesses in your industry that complement what you do. For example, if you're a web designer, you could partner with a digital marketing agency.

You can also search for businesses that serve the same target market as you but offer different products or services. For example, if you sell women's clothing, you could partner with a jewelry store or a hair salon.

Bottom Line

Starting a small business takes time, effort and perseverance. But if you're willing to put in the work, it can be a great way to achieve your dreams and goals. Be sure to do your research, create a solid business plan and pivot along the way. Once you're operational, don't forget to stay focused and organized so you can continue to grow your business.

Determining Entrepreneurial Success

Entrepreneurial success is a multifaceted concept that goes beyond financial achievements. It encompasses a combination of factors, including personal fulfillment, impact on society, and the ability to adapt and thrive in a competitive marketplace. While the definition of success may vary from one entrepreneur to another, there are common elements that contribute to determining success in the entrepreneurial realm. In this discussion, we will explore the key factors that play a role in determining entrepreneurial success and shed light on the mindset and strategies that entrepreneurs can employ to achieve their goals.

1. Clear Vision and Defined Goals

Entrepreneurial success begins with a clear vision and defined goals. Successful entrepreneurs possess a strong sense of purpose and a deep understanding of what they want to achieve. They have a clear vision of their business and can articulate their goals in a concise and compelling manner. This clarity of vision serves as a guiding force, providing focus and direction seefor their actions and decisions.

2. Passion and Perseverance

Passion is a driving force behind entrepreneurial success. Successful entrepreneurs are deeply passionate about their business and the impact they can create. They are willing to put in the hard work, face challenges head-on, and persevere in the face of adversity. Passion fuels their determination and helps them overcome obstacles that come their way.

3. Adaptability and Continuous Learning

In today's fast-paced and ever-changing business landscape, adaptability is crucial for entrepreneurial success. Successful entrepreneurs are quick to embrace change and are open to new ideas and perspectives. They continuously seek opportunities for growth and improvement, and they are willing to learn from their experiences and mistakes. Adaptability allows entrepreneurs to stay ahead of the curve, navigate challenges, and capitalize on emerging trends.

4. Innovation and Creativity

Entrepreneurial success often stems from innovation and creativity. Successful entrepreneurs have a knack for identifying unmet needs, gaps in the market, and innovative solutions. They constantly seek ways to differentiate themselves from the competition and create unique value propositions. Innovation and creativity enable entrepreneurs to develop groundbreaking products, services, and business models that disrupt industries and captivate customers.

5. Customer Focus and Market Understanding

Understanding the target market and meeting customer needs is crucial for entrepreneurial success. Successful entrepreneurs prioritize customer satisfaction and go the extra mile to deliver exceptional experiences. They conduct market research, gather customer feedback, and adapt their offerings accordingly. By deeply understanding their customers and their pain points, entrepreneurs can develop products and services that truly resonate with their target audience.

6. Building Strong Networks and Collaborations

Entrepreneurial success is often influenced by the strength of one's network and the ability to form strategic collaborations. Successful entrepreneurs recognize the value of building relationships with mentors, industry experts, and potential partners. They actively seek opportunities to network, attend industry events, and join entrepreneurial communities. Strong networks and collaborations provide access to resources, knowledge, and opportunities that can accelerate business growth.

7. Financial Management and Sustainability

Financial management is a critical aspect of entrepreneurial success. Successful entrepreneurs understand the importance of effective financial planning, budgeting, and resource allocation. They carefully manage cash flow, monitor expenses, and make informed financial decisions. Additionally, sustainable business practices and responsible resource management contribute to long-term success, ensuring the business can weather economic downturns and remain resilient.

8. Leadership and Team Building

Entrepreneurial success relies heavily on effective leadership and team building. Successful entrepreneurs possess strong leadership skills and the ability to inspire and motivate their teams. They surround themselves with talented individuals who share their vision and values. By fostering a positive work culture, empowering their employees, and nurturing talent, entrepreneurs can build high-performing teams that drive business success.

9. Resilience and Adaptation to Failure

Failure is an inevitable part of the entrepreneurial journey, and resilience is crucial in overcoming setbacks.

Vision and Passion are Important

Vision and passion are two essential elements that drive entrepreneurial success. They are the fuel that ignites the entrepreneurial journey, propels individuals forward, and sustains their motivation in the face of challenges and setbacks. A strong vision provides a sense of purpose and direction, while passion fuels the drive and commitment necessary to transform ideas into reality. In this discussion, we will delve into the significance of vision and passion in entrepreneurial success and explore how they shape the mindset, decision-making, and actions of successful entrepreneurs.

1. Vision: Charting the Path to Success

A clear and compelling vision is the foundation upon which successful businesses are built. It is the guiding force that shapes the direction, goals, and strategies of an entrepreneurial venture. A strong vision serves as a roadmap, providing clarity and focus amidst the uncertainties of the business landscape. It allows entrepreneurs to articulate their purpose and communicate their mission to stakeholders, including employees, investors, and customers.

A well-defined vision creates a sense of unity and alignment within the organization, rallying team members around a common goal. It provides a framework for decision-making, enabling entrepreneurs to prioritize activities and allocate resources effectively. Moreover, a vision inspires creativity and innovation, encouraging entrepreneurs to think outside the box and explore new possibilities.

2. Passion: Fueling the Entrepreneurial Fire

Passion is the driving force behind entrepreneurial success. It is the unwavering enthusiasm and emotional connection that entrepreneurs have with their business and its purpose. Passion fuels the relentless pursuit of goals, propelling individuals to overcome obstacles, take risks, and persist in the face of adversity. It provides the resilience necessary to bounce back from failures and setbacks, transforming them into valuable learning experiences.

Entrepreneurs who are passionate about their business exude infectious energy and inspire those around them. They are willing to put in the long hours and hard work required to bring their vision to life. Passion fuels creativity, encouraging entrepreneurs to innovate and differentiate themselves in a crowded marketplace. It also fosters a deep sense of commitment to delivering value to customers, driving the pursuit of excellence in product or service offerings.

3. Aligning Vision and Passion

The true power of vision and passion lies in their alignment. When vision and passion are harmonized, entrepreneurs are equipped with a compelling force that propels them forward and enables them to overcome obstacles. A well-aligned vision and passion create a sense of purpose that goes beyond financial gains, driving entrepreneurs to create meaningful and impactful businesses.

Entrepreneurs who align their passion with their vision are more likely to persevere during challenging times. They are driven by a higher purpose, allowing them to maintain focus and motivation, even in the face of adversity. Their passion becomes a source of inspiration for employees and stakeholders, fostering a shared commitment to the vision and mission of the business.

4. Sustaining Vision and Passion

Sustaining vision and passion over the long term is essential for entrepreneurial success. To maintain their vision, entrepreneurs must regularly revisit and refine it as the business evolves. They must stay attuned to changing market dynamics and customer needs, ensuring that their vision remains relevant and aligned with emerging trends.

Similarly, sustaining passion requires continuous self-reflection and renewal. Entrepreneurs must nurture their passion by engaging in activities that fuel their enthusiasm, such as networking with like-minded individuals, seeking mentorship, and pursuing personal growth. They must also cultivate a supportive environment that fosters creativity, innovation, and a sense of purpose within the organization.

Chapter 2:

Starting from the Ground Up: Laying the Groundwork.

Building a successful business from the ground up is a challenging yet rewarding journey. It requires careful planning, meticulous execution, and a solid foundation to support future growth. Laying the groundwork involves establishing the necessary infrastructure, developing a robust business plan, and cultivating a strong entrepreneurial mindset. In this discussion, we will explore the crucial steps involved in starting a business from scratch and setting the stage for long-term success.

1. Identifying a Viable Business Idea

The first step in laying the groundwork for a successful business is identifying a viable business idea. This involves conducting market research to identify gaps, trends, and opportunities in the target industry. Entrepreneurs must assess the demand for their product or service, understand the competitive landscape, and determine their unique value proposition. By conducting thorough market research, entrepreneurs can ensure that their business idea has the potential for success and addresses a genuine customer need.

2. Developing a Solid Business Plan

A well-crafted business plan is essential for laying the groundwork and attracting investors or securing financing. It outlines the company's mission, vision, and objectives, as well as the strategies and tactics to achieve them. A comprehensive business plan includes market analysis, competitive analysis, marketing strategies, financial projections, and an operational plan. This plan serves as a roadmap, providing guidance for the early stages of the business and setting the stage for future growth.

3. Building a Strong Team

A successful business is built on the foundation of a strong and dedicated team. Entrepreneurs should carefully select individuals who share their vision, possess the necessary skills, and complement their own strengths and weaknesses. Building a strong team involves recruiting, hiring, and retaining talented individuals who are passionate about the company's mission. Additionally, entrepreneurs should foster a positive work culture that encourages collaboration, innovation, and continuous learning.

4. Securing Adequate Funding

Securing adequate funding is crucial for laying the groundwork and sustaining the business during its early stages. Entrepreneurs can explore various funding options, including personal savings, loans, grants, crowdfunding, or seeking investment from venture capitalists or angel investors. It is essential to have a clear understanding of the financial needs of the business and develop a comprehensive financial plan that outlines the use of funds and projected revenue streams.

5. Establishing Legal and Administrative Framework

To ensure compliance and protect the business, entrepreneurs must establish a solid legal and administrative framework. This includes registering the business, obtaining the necessary licenses and permits, and setting up appropriate legal structures such as a sole proprietorship, partnership, or limited liability company (LLC). Entrepreneurs should also establish clear policies and procedures, such as employment contracts, confidentiality agreements, and intellectual property protection, to safeguard their assets and interests.

6. Creating a Brand Identity

Building a strong brand identity is essential for laying the groundwork and differentiating the business in the marketplace. Entrepreneurs should develop a compelling brand strategy that encompasses the company's values, mission, and unique selling propositions. This involves creating a memorable brand name, designing a visually appealing logo, and developing consistent messaging across all marketing channels. By establishing a strong brand presence, entrepreneurs can attract customers, build trust, and establish a competitive edge.

7. Developing Marketing and Sales Strategies

An effective marketing and sales strategy is critical for laying the groundwork and generating initial customer interest. Entrepreneurs should identify their target audience, understand their needs and preferences, and tailor their marketing efforts accordingly. This may include leveraging digital marketing channels, creating engaging content, utilizing social media platforms, and exploring traditional advertising methods. Developing a solid sales strategy involves defining pricing models, building sales pipelines, and establishing effective customer acquisition and retention tactics.

8. Embracing an Entrepreneurial

Lastly, laying the groundwork for a successful business requires embracing an entrepreneurial mindset. This mindset involves adopting a proactive and opportunistic approach to challenges and opportunities. Entrepreneurs must be willing to take calculated risks, embrace uncertainty, and learn from failures. They should possess a growth mindset, constantly seeking opportunities for personal and professional development.An entrepreneurial mindset also involves being adaptable, agile, and open to new ideas and feedback. By cultivating this mindset, entrepreneurs can navigate the complexities of starting a business and overcome obstacles with resilience and determination.

Finding a Profitable Business Idea

The foundation of any successful business lies in identifying a profitable business idea. However, finding the right idea that not only aligns with your interests and skills but also has the potential to generate sustainable profits can be a daunting task. It requires a combination of creativity, market research, and strategic thinking. In this discussion, we will explore the key steps and considerations involved in finding a profitable business idea and maximizing your chances of entrepreneurial success.

1. Identify Your Passion and Skills

To start the journey of finding a profitable business idea, it is important to begin with self-reflection. Consider your passions, interests, and skills. What are you truly passionate about? What expertise or skills do you possess? By aligning your business idea with your passion and skills, you are more likely to stay motivated, committed, and invested in the long run. This foundation of passion and expertise will drive your success and allow you to differentiate yourself from competitors.

2. Conduct Market Research

Market research plays a crucial role in identifying a profitable business idea. It helps you understand the market dynamics, customer needs, and existing competition. Start by analyzing industry trends and growth potential. Look for gaps in the market where there is unmet demand or underserved customer segments. Explore emerging trends and technologies that can be leveraged to create innovative solutions.

Next, conduct target market research to gain insights into the preferences, behaviors, and pain points of your potential customers. This can be done through surveys, interviews, and online research. Understanding your target market's needs and desires will enable you to develop products or services that truly resonate with them.

Additionally, analyze your competitors. Study their offerings, pricing strategies, marketing approaches, and customer feedback. Identify areas where you can differentiate yourself and provide unique value to customers. By conducting comprehensive market research, you can uncover lucrative opportunities and develop a solid understanding of the market landscape.

3. Identify Problems and Solutions

Successful businesses often revolve around solving problems and meeting unmet needs. Look for pain points or inefficiencies in existing products or services. Ask yourself what challenges people face in their daily lives or what frustrations they encounter. Consider how you can provide solutions or improve upon existing offerings. This problem-solving approach can lead to the development of a profitable business idea.

Brainstorm ideas that address these problems or fulfill unmet needs. Generate multiple ideas and evaluate their feasibility, scalability, and potential profitability. Assess the demand, market size, and revenue potential for each idea. Narrow down your options to the most promising ones that align with your passion and skills and have the highest potential for profitability.

4. Test and Validate Your Idea

Once you have identified a potential business idea, it is important to test and validate its viability before fully committing to it. This involves conducting market tests and seeking feedback from your target audience. Create prototypes or minimum viable products (MVPs) to gather real-world feedback and assess the market response.

Engage with potential customers through surveys, focus groups, or beta testing. Gather their feedback, understand their preferences, and make necessary iterations to refine your idea. This iterative process of testing and validation helps ensure that your business idea resonates with the market and has the potential to generate profits.

5. Consider Scalability and Profitability

When evaluating a business idea, consider its scalability and profitability potential. Scalability refers to the ability of a business to grow and expand without being limited by resources or operational constraints. Assess whether your business idea can be easily scaled and whether there is a significant market demand that can sustain its growth.

Profitability is another critical factor. Evaluate the potential revenue streams, cost structures, and profit margins associated with your business idea. Consider the pricing strategies, operational efficiencies, and cost-saving measures that can maximize profitability. A profitable business idea should have

the potential to generate sustainable revenue and deliver a return on investment.

6. Stay Open to Opportunities and Adaptation

While it is important to have a clear business idea, it is equally important to stay open to new opportunities and adapt to changing market dynamics. Keep an eye on industry trends, emerging technologies, and shifting consumer preferences. Be willing to pivot or refine your business idea if necessary to stay relevant and seize new opportunities.

Establishing a Strong Network

In the world of entrepreneurship, establishing a strong network is essential for success. Building meaningful relationships with like-minded individuals, industry professionals, mentors, and potential customers can open doors to new opportunities, provide valuable guidance and support, and help propel your business forward. A strong network not only offers access to resources and knowledge but also creates a support system that can help navigate the challenges of entrepreneurship. In this discussion, we will explore the importance of establishing a strong network and provide insights on how to build and leverage it effectively.

Expand Your Reach

One of the primary benefits of establishing a strong network is the ability to expand your reach. By connecting with individuals from diverse backgrounds and industries, you gain access to a wider pool of knowledge, experiences, and perspectives. This expanded reach can spark creativity, inspire innovation, and provide fresh insights into your business and industry.

Attend industry conferences, seminars, and networking events to meet professionals and entrepreneurs in your field. Engage in online communities, join relevant social media groups, and participate in forums where you can connect with like-minded individuals and experts. By actively seeking out opportunities to expand your reach, you increase your chances of finding valuable connections and building a strong network.

Seek Mentorship and Guidance

Establishing relationships with experienced mentors can provide invaluable guidance and support on your entrepreneurial journey. Mentors can share their knowledge, offer practical advice, and help you navigate challenges based on their own experiences. They can provide insights into industry trends, introduce you to key contacts, and help you avoid common pitfalls.

Look for mentors who have expertise in your field or have successfully built businesses similar to what you aspire to achieve. Attend networking events or join mentorship programs specifically designed to connect entrepreneurs with seasoned professionals. When approaching potential mentors, be respectful of their time and demonstrate your commitment and enthusiasm for learning from them. A strong mentorship relationship can accelerate your personal and professional growth, giving you a competitive advantage in your entrepreneurial endeavors.

Cultivate Meaningful Relationships

Building a strong network goes beyond simply collecting business cards or adding contacts to your LinkedIn profile. It is about cultivating meaningful relationships based on trust, respect, and mutual support. Take the time to get to know the individuals in your network on a deeper level, understand their goals, and find ways to support and add value to their endeavors.

Regularly engage with your network by attending industry events, organizing meetups or gatherings, and staying in touch through emails or social media. Offer your expertise, provide assistance when needed, and share relevant resources or connections. By actively contributing to the success of others in your network, you establish yourself as a valuable and reliable contact, increasing the likelihood of reciprocation and building long-lasting relationships.

Leverage Online Platforms and Communities

In today's digital age, online platforms and communities provide excellent opportunities to build and expand your network. Social media platforms such as LinkedIn, Twitter, and Facebook offer avenues to connect with professionals, industry leaders, and potential customers. Join industry-specific online communities, participate in discussions, and contribute valuable insights to establish your presence and credibility.

Additionally, consider starting your own blog or podcast to share your expertise and attract individuals with similar interests. These platforms can help you reach a broader audience and establish yourself as a thought leader in your industry. Actively engage with your online network, respond to comments and messages, and take advantage of the digital landscape to foster meaningful connections.

Give and Receive Support

A strong network is a two-way street, and it is essential to both give and receive support. Be willing to offer your help, advice, or connections when someone in your network is in need. Providing assistance without expecting immediate returns builds trust and strengthens the bonds within your network.

Chapter 3

The Execution Power: Making Ideas a Reality

Having a brilliant idea is just the beginning of the entrepreneurial journey. The true measure of success lies in the execution of that idea. Many aspiring entrepreneurs have great ideas, but only a few are able to turn them into reality. The ability to execute effectively and efficiently is what sets successful businesses apart. In this discussion, we will explore the concept of execution power and highlight key strategies for bringing ideas to life and achieving entrepreneurial success.

1. Develop a Clear Plan

Execution starts with a clear and well-defined plan. Outline the specific steps required to turn your idea into a tangible product or service. Break down the plan into manageable tasks and set clear objectives and milestones. By having a roadmap, you provide yourself with a sense of direction and ensure that you stay focused and on track.

Consider creating a detailed project plan or using project management tools to organize and track your progress. Clearly define roles and responsibilities, set deadlines, and allocate resources effectively. A well-developed plan not only helps you stay organized but also provides a framework for measuring your progress and making necessary adjustments along the way.

2. Prioritize and Take Action

Execution requires prioritization and taking action. With limited time and resources, it is essential to identify the most critical tasks and focus your efforts on them. Determine which actions will have the greatest impact on your business and prioritize them accordingly. By focusing on high-value tasks, you can make the most efficient use of your resources and move closer to your goals.

Avoid falling into the trap of analysis paralysis, where you spend excessive time planning without taking action. While planning is important, ultimately, it is the execution that matters. Be willing to take calculated risks, make decisions, and take decisive action. Embrace a mindset of progress over perfection, understanding that it is better to make progress and iterate than to wait for the perfect conditions.

3. Build a Strong Team

Execution is a team effort. Surround yourself with talented individuals who share your vision and possess the necessary skills to execute your plan. Delegate tasks and empower your team members to take ownership of their responsibilities. A strong team can provide valuable support, diverse perspectives, and expertise in different areas, helping you execute more effectively.

Invest time and effort in hiring the right people who align with your values and have the skills required to contribute to your business. Foster a collaborative and supportive work culture where open communication and constructive feedback are encouraged. By building a strong team, you create a foundation for successful execution and enable your business to thrive.

4. Embrace Agile and Iterative Approach

Execution is not a linear process. It often requires flexibility and adaptability. Embrace an agile and iterative approach, where you continuously evaluate and adjust your strategies based on feedback and changing circumstances. Test your assumptions, gather data, and make informed decisions accordingly.

Breaking down your plan into smaller, manageable tasks allows for frequent iterations and adjustments. Regularly review your progress, gather feedback from customers and stakeholders, and use that information to refine your strategies and tactics. By embracing an iterative approach, you can make course corrections early on, avoid potential pitfalls, and optimize your execution.

5. Stay Focused and Persevere

Execution requires focus and perseverance. It is easy to get distracted or discouraged when faced with challenges and setbacks. However, successful entrepreneurs understand that setbacks are a natural part of the journey. Stay focused on your long-term vision and goals, and remain determined in the face of adversity.

Develop resilience and the ability to learn from failures. Use setbacks as opportunities for growth and improvement. Celebrate small victories along the way to maintain motivation and momentum. Remember that execution is a marathon, not a sprint. It requires consistency, discipline, and a commitment to seeing your ideas through to fruition.

Obtaining the Initial Funding and Resources

When starting a business, one of the most crucial aspects is obtaining the initial funding and resources necessary to turn your ideas into a reality. Whether it's securing capital to cover startup costs, acquiring essential equipment and materials, or establishing a strong network of support, having access to the right resources is vital for launching and growing a successful venture. In this discussion, we will explore the strategies and avenues entrepreneurs can pursue to obtain the initial funding and resources needed to kickstart their business endeavors.

1. Self-Funding and Bootstrapping

Self-funding, also known as bootstrapping, is a common approach where entrepreneurs use their personal savings or assets to finance their business. This method allows entrepreneurs to maintain control over their business and avoids the need to rely on external sources of funding. By leveraging personal funds, entrepreneurs have the flexibility to make decisions and allocate resources as they see fit.

Bootstrapping requires careful financial planning and disciplined spending. It often involves starting small, being resourceful, and maximizing efficiency. This may include working from home, minimizing overhead costs, or leveraging existing networks for support and collaboration. While bootstrapping may have limitations in terms of the scale of growth, it provides entrepreneurs with a sense of independence and ownership.

2. Friends and Family

Another common source of initial funding for entrepreneurs is friends and family. This involves seeking financial support from close acquaintances, such as relatives, friends, or mentors, who believe in the entrepreneur's vision and are willing to invest in their business. Friends and family can provide the initial capital needed to get the business off the ground and often offer more flexible terms compared to traditional lenders or investors.

When approaching friends and family for funding, it is crucial to treat the arrangement professionally. Clearly define the terms of the investment, including the amount, repayment structure, and any equity or ownership arrangements. It is also important to consider the potential impact on personal relationships and have open and transparent communication about the risks involved. While funding from friends and family can be a valuable resource, it is essential to manage expectations and ensure that all parties are aligned.

3. Small Business Loans and Grants

Small business loans and grants are viable options for entrepreneurs seeking external funding. These financial resources are typically provided by banks, financial institutions, government agencies, or non-profit organizations. Small business loans are structured as debt that needs to be repaid over time, usually with interest. Grants, on the other hand, do not require repayment and are often awarded based on specific eligibility criteria and objectives.

When applying for loans or grants, it is important to have a solid business plan, financial projections, and a clear understanding of the requirements and obligations associated with the funding. Research available options and eligibility criteria to identify the most suitable programs for your business. Seek professional guidance or utilize resources provided by Small Business Administration (SBA) or local business development centers to navigate the application process effectively.

4. Crowdfunding

Crowdfunding has gained significant popularity in recent years as a means of obtaining initial funding for businesses. It involves raising small amounts of money from a large number of individuals, typically through online platforms. Crowdfunding allows entrepreneurs to showcase their business idea or product to a broad audience and attract potential backers who are interested in supporting their venture.

There are different types of crowdfunding models, including donation-based, rewards-based, equity-based, and debt-based. Each model has its own set of rules and regulations, and entrepreneurs should carefully consider the implications and obligations associated with the chosen model. Crowdfunding requires effective marketing and communication strategies to engage potential backers and create a compelling campaign that resonates with the audience.

5. Angel Investors and Venture Capitalists

For businesses with high growth potential, seeking funding from angel investors or venture capitalists can be an option. Angel investors are individuals who provide funding to early-stage businesses in exchange for equity or ownership stake. They often bring industry expertise and mentorship to the table. Venture capitalists, on the other hand, are professional investment firms that provide capital to startups in exchange for equity with the goal of high returns on their investment.

When approaching angel investors or venture capitalists, entrepreneurs need to demonstrate a strong business model, a compelling value proposition, and a scalable growth strategy. It is essential to thoroughly research and target investors who have a track record of investing in businesses similar to yours. Networking events, pitch competitions, and industry conferences can provide opportunities to connect with potential investors and showcase your business.

6. Strategic Partnerships and Alliances

Establishing strategic partnerships and alliances can be a valuable way to access resources and funding. Collaborating with established companies or organizations that have complementary products, services, or customer bases can provide a range of benefits. This can include shared marketing efforts, access to distribution channels, or financial support.

Identify potential partners or alliances that align with your business objectives and reach out to explore mutually beneficial opportunities. Building relationships based on trust and shared goals can lead to long-term partnerships that provide access to funding, expertise, and a broader customer base.

7. Incubators and Accelerators

Incubators and accelerators are programs designed to support early-stage startups by providing a range of resources and services. These programs offer mentorship, workspace, access to networks, and sometimes even funding. Incubators tend to have a longer-term focus on nurturing and developing startups, while accelerators have a more intensive and time-limited program that aims to rapidly accelerate growth.

Research and apply to reputable incubator or accelerator programs that align with your industry and business goals. These programs often require a competitive application process, but the benefits of access to resources, mentorship, and potential funding can greatly enhance the prospects of your business.

8. Tap into Personal and Professional Networks

Never underestimate the power of your personal and professional networks. Your existing connections can be a valuable source of support, advice, and even funding. Reach out to individuals who may be interested in investing or providing resources based on their belief in your abilities and the potential of your business.

Attend industry events, join networking groups, and actively engage with your network to build relationships and seek opportunities. Utilize online platforms such as LinkedIn to expand your professional network and connect with individuals who can provide guidance and support.

•Obtaining the initial funding and resources is a critical step in the entrepreneurial journey. From self-funding and bootstrapping to seeking support from friends and family, exploring small business loans and grants, leveraging crowdfunding, attracting angel investors or venture capitalists, establishing strategic partnerships, and tapping into incubators and accelerators, there are numerous avenues to consider.

Every entrepreneur's journey is unique, and the funding and resource acquisition process will vary depending on factors such as the nature of the business, industry, and growth potential. It is important to conduct thorough research, develop a clear funding strategy, and tailor your approach to align with your business goals.

Remember that securing the initial funding is just the beginning. Once you have obtained the necessary resources, it is essential to manage them effectively, monitor your financial closely, and utilize the acquired resources wisely to drive the growth and success of your business.

Chapter 4:

Marketing and Sales Strategies for Navigating the Competitive Landscape

In today's competitive business environment, effective marketing and sales strategies are crucial for the success of any venture. Navigating the competitive landscape requires a comprehensive approach that enables businesses to stand out, reach their target audience, and convert prospects into loyal customers. In this discussion, we will explore key marketing and sales strategies that entrepreneurs can employ to gain a competitive edge and achieve sustainable growth.

1. Identify and Understand Your Target Market

Before implementing any marketing or sales strategy, it is essential to identify and understand your target market. Conduct thorough market research to gain insights into your customers' demographics, preferences, needs, and pain points. This information will enable you to tailor your marketing messages and sales approach to resonate with your target audience.

Segment your market into distinct customer groups and develop buyer personas that represent your ideal customers. This will help you create targeted marketing campaigns and sales strategies that are specifically tailored to address the unique needs and motivations of each customer segment.

2. Build a Strong Brand

Building a strong brand is a critical aspect of marketing and sales success. A well-defined brand identity sets you apart from competitors and establishes a connection with your target audience. Develop a compelling brand story that communicates your mission, values, and unique selling proposition.

Invest in creating a visually appealing and consistent brand image across all marketing channels. This includes your logo, website, social media profiles, packaging, and any other touchpoints with customers. Consistency in messaging and design builds trust and reinforces your brand in the minds of your customers.

3. Develop an Effective Digital Marketing Strategy

In today's digital age, a strong online presence is essential for businesses to thrive. Develop a comprehensive digital marketing strategy that encompasses various channels such as search engine optimization (SEO), content marketing, social media marketing, email marketing, and paid advertising.

Optimize your website to rank higher in search engine results, create valuable and engaging content that educates and entertains your target audience, leverage social media platforms to connect with and engage customers, and utilize email marketing to nurture leads and build customer relationships. Paid advertising, such as search engine marketing or social media advertising, can also be effective in reaching a wider audience and driving targeted traffic to your website.

4. Leverage Social Proof and Customer Reviews

In a competitive landscape, social proof and customer reviews play a crucial role in influencing purchasing decisions. Encourage your satisfied customers to leave reviews and testimonials about their positive experiences with your product or service. Display these reviews prominently on your website and social media platforms to build trust and credibility.

Additionally, consider partnering with influencers or industry experts who can endorse your brand and products. Their influence and positive recommendations can significantly impact the perception of your business and attract new customers.

5. Implement Effective Sales Strategies

Marketing efforts must be supported by effective sales strategies to convert leads into customers. Train your sales team to effectively communicate the value of your products or services and address customer concerns. Develop a sales process that guides your team through each stage of the customer journey, from initial contact to closing the sale.

Consider implementing sales techniques such as upselling and cross-selling to maximize revenue from each customer. Offer personalized solutions and incentives to encourage repeat purchases and customer loyalty. Provide exceptional customer service to ensure customer satisfaction and foster long-term relationships.

6. Monitor and Analyze Data

Data analysis is critical for evaluating the effectiveness of your marketing and sales efforts. Implement analytics tools to track key performance indicators (KPIs) such as website traffic, conversion rates, customer acquisition cost, and customer lifetime value. This data will help you identify areas of improvement, optimize your strategies, and make data-driven decisions.

Regularly review your marketing and sales metrics to identify trends and patterns. Use A/B testing to experiment with different marketing messages, designs, and strategies to determine what resonates best with your target audience. By continually monitoring and analyzing data, you can refine your marketing and sales strategies, allocate resources effectively, and stay ahead of the competition.

Establishing a Brand Identity

In the business world, establishing a strong brand identity is vital for success. A brand identity goes beyond a company's logo and visual elements; it encompasses the values, personality, and essence of a business. It is the foundation upon which all marketing and communication efforts are built. In this discussion, we will explore the key elements and strategies involved in establishing a compelling brand identity.

1. Define Your Brand Purpose and Values

At the core of a brand identity is a clear understanding of the brand's purpose and values. Define the purpose of your business beyond making profits. What drives your company? What problem does it solve? What values and principles guide your decisions and actions?

By articulating your brand's purpose and values, you create a foundation that resonates with your target audience. Customers are increasingly drawn to brands that align with their values and beliefs. Establishing a strong brand purpose and values sets the tone for your brand identity and shapes the perception of your business in the minds of consumers.

2. Understand Your Target Audience

To establish a brand identity that connects with your target audience, it is essential to understand their needs, desires, and preferences. Conduct market research, analyze customer demographics, and identify key characteristics of your target audience. What motivates them? What are their pain points? What do they look for in a brand?

This deep understanding allows you to tailor your brand identity to resonate with your target audience. It influences the language, tone, and visual elements that you use to communicate with them. By speaking their language and addressing their needs, you can build a strong emotional connection and loyalty.

3. Craft a Unique Value Proposition

In a crowded marketplace, a unique value proposition sets your brand apart from competitors. Identify what makes your business unique and how it brings value to customers. Is it exceptional quality, superior customer service, innovative solutions, or a combination of factors?

Communicate your unique value proposition clearly and consistently in your brand messaging. Whether it's through your tagline, website copy, or social media content, highlight the benefits and advantages that customers can expect when engaging with your brand. Your value proposition should resonate with your target audience and give them a compelling reason to choose your brand over others.

4. Develop a Distinctive Visual Identity

Visual elements play a crucial role in establishing a brand identity. Your logo, color palette, typography, and overall design aesthetics should be carefully considered and aligned with your brand's personality and values. These elements evoke emotions and create recognition and recall.

Invest in professional graphic design services to ensure that your visual identity is cohesive, visually appealing, and memorable. Consistency across all brand touchpoints, including your website, packaging, marketing materials, and social media profiles, is key to reinforcing your brand identity.

5. Craft a Consistent Brand Voice and Tone

Your brand voice and tone encompass the language and style in which you communicate with your audience. It should be consistent across all channels and reflect the personality and values of your brand. Consider whether your brand voice is formal, casual, friendly, authoritative, or playful, depending on your target audience and industry.

Consistency in brand voice and tone helps build trust and familiarity with your audience. Whether it's through social media posts, blog articles, or customer interactions, maintain a consistent voice that aligns with your brand identity. It should be reflective of your values and resonate with your target audience.

6. Deliver Consistent Brand Experiences

Brand identity is not limited to visual and verbal elements; it also encompasses the overall experience customers have with your brand. Every touchpoint, from the moment a customer interacts with your brand to their post-purchase experience, contributes to the perception of your brand.

Consistency in delivering brand experiences builds trust and credibility. Ensure that your customer service, product quality, packaging, and overall brand experience align with your brand identity to create a cohesive and memorable impression.

Putting Effective Sales Strategies in Place

Sales strategies play a crucial role in the success of any business. They guide the process of converting prospects into customers and ultimately driving revenue. To achieve sustainable growth, it is essential to put effective sales strategies in place. In this discussion, we will explore key elements and best practices for developing and implementing successful sales strategies.

1. Set Clear Sales Objectives

The first step in putting effective sales strategies in place is to set clear objectives. Define what you want to achieve with your sales efforts, such as revenue targets, market share growth, or customer acquisition goals. Setting specific, measurable, achievable, relevant, and time-bound (SMART) objectives provides a clear direction for your sales team and enables you to track progress and success.

2. Know Your Target Market

To effectively sell your products or services, it is crucial to understand your target market. Conduct market research to identify your ideal customers, their needs, pain points, and buying behavior. Develop buyer personas that represent your target audience segments, and tailor your sales strategies to address their specific needs and motivations.

By understanding your target market, you can position your offering as a solution to their problems, customize your sales approach, and communicate the value of your product or service effectively.

3. Train and Equip Your Sales Team

Your sales team is at the forefront of your sales efforts. Invest in training and equipping them with the skills and knowledge necessary to succeed. Provide ongoing training on effective sales techniques, product knowledge, objection handling, and relationship building.

Additionally, provide your sales team with the necessary tools and resources to streamline their sales process. This includes CRM systems, sales enablement software, marketing collateral, and competitive intelligence. Empower your team with the right information and tools to effectively engage with prospects and close deals.

4. Develop a Sales Process

A well-defined sales process is essential for consistency and efficiency in your sales efforts. Develop a step-by-step process that outlines the stages from prospecting to closing the sale. This process should align with your customers' buying journey and include activities such as lead generation, qualification, needs analysis, presentation, negotiation, and closing.

Regularly review and refine your sales process based on customer feedback and market dynamics. Continuously optimize the process to ensure it remains effective in meeting your sales objectives.

5. Foster Relationship Building

Building strong relationships with prospects and customers is a key aspect of successful sales strategies. Focus on understanding their needs, actively listening to their concerns, and providing personalized solutions. Develop a consultative approach, where you position yourself as a trusted advisor rather than a pushy salesperson.

Maintain regular communication with your prospects and customers, even beyond the initial sale. Nurture relationships through follow-ups, providing valuable insights, and offering ongoing support. Strong relationships lead to customer loyalty, repeat business, and positive referrals.

6. Leverage Technology and Automation

Technology and automation can significantly enhance your sales strategies. Utilize customer relationship management (CRM) software to manage customer data, track sales activities, and gain insights into customer behavior. Automation tools can streamline repetitive tasks, such as email campaigns, lead scoring, and appointment scheduling.

By leveraging technology and automation, you can improve productivity, optimize sales processes, and ensure that leads are effectively managed and nurtured.

7. Measure and Analyze Performance

Measuring and analyzing sales performance is crucial for identifying strengths, weaknesses, and opportunities for improvement. Establish key performance indicators (KPIs) to track progress and evaluate the effectiveness of your sales strategies. Common KPIs include conversion rates, average deal size, sales cycle length, and customer lifetime value.

Regularly analyze sales data to identify trends, patterns, and areas for improvement. Use this information to refine your sales strategies, address bottlenecks, and allocate resources effectively.

Making Use of Digital Marketing and Social Media

In today's digital age, businesses need to leverage digital marketing and social media platforms to effectively reach and engage their target audience. Digital marketing offers a wide range of tools and strategies that can help businesses expand their reach, drive traffic, generate leads, and ultimately increase conversions. In this discussion, we will explore the importance of digital marketing and social media and discuss key strategies for making the most of these platforms.

1. Embrace a Comprehensive Digital Marketing Strategy

A comprehensive digital marketing strategy encompasses various channels and tactics to maximize your online presence. Begin by understanding your target audience and their online behavior. This will help you identify the most effective channels to reach them, whether it's search engines, social media platforms, email marketing, content marketing, or paid advertising.

Develop a cohesive strategy that integrates different digital marketing components. For instance, optimize your website for search engines through search engine optimization (SEO), create valuable and relevant content to engage and educate your audience, leverage social media platforms to build brand awareness and engage with customers, and utilize email marketing to nurture leads and drive conversions.

2. Utilize Search Engine Optimization (SEO)

Search engine optimization is the process of improving your website's visibility in search engine results pages. By optimizing your website for relevant keywords and implementing other SEO techniques, you can increase organic traffic and attract qualified leads. Conduct keyword research to identify the terms and phrases your target audience is searching for, and strategically incorporate them into your website's content, meta tags, and URLs.

Additionally, focus on technical SEO aspects such as website speed, mobile optimization, and user-friendly navigation. Regularly monitor and analyze your website's performance using analytics tools to identify areas for improvement and refine your SEO strategy.

3. Engage with Social Media Platforms

Social media platforms offer a powerful way to connect with your target audience, build brand awareness, and foster customer engagement. Identify the social media platforms that are most popular among your target audience, and develop a content strategy that aligns with the unique characteristics of each platform.

Regularly post relevant and engaging content that resonates with your audience, such as articles, videos, infographics, and user-generated content. Encourage social sharing and interaction by responding to comments, initiating discussions, and running contests or giveaways. Social media also provides an opportunity for targeted advertising, allowing you to reach specific demographics and interests with precision.

4. Implement Content Marketing

Content marketing involves creating and distributing valuable and relevant content to attract and retain a clearly defined audience. Develop a content strategy that aligns with your target audience's interests, needs, and pain points. Create high-quality blog articles, e-books, videos, podcasts, and other forms of content that provide value to your audience.

Share your content across various channels, including your website, blog, social media platforms, and email newsletters. Consistently producing valuable content establishes your brand as a thought leader in your industry, builds trust with your audience, and increases brand visibility.

5. Leverage Email Marketing

Email marketing remains one of the most effective ways to nurture leads and drive conversions. Build an email list by offering valuable incentives such as e-books, discounts, or exclusive content in exchange for visitors' email addresses. Segment your email list based on demographics, interests, and purchasing behavior to deliver targeted and personalized content.

Craft compelling email campaigns that provide value to your subscribers, such as product updates, industry news, educational content, and special offers. Use automation tools to set up drip campaigns, triggered emails, and personalized follow-ups based on user actions or specific time intervals.

6. Incorporate Pay-Per-Click (PPC) Advertising

Pay-per-click advertising allows businesses to display ads on search engines and other digital platforms and pay only when a user clicks on the ad. PPC advertising provided a cost effective way to reach a targeted audience, increase brand visibility, and drive traffic to your website or landing pages.

Chapter 5:

Expanding and Scaling the Business

Once a business has established a solid foundation and achieved initial success, the next step is to focus on expanding and scaling operations. Expanding a business involves reaching new markets, introducing new products or services, and diversifying revenue streams. Scaling, on the other hand, involves increasing operational capacity to accommodate growing demand. In this discussion, we will explore key strategies and considerations for expanding and scaling a business.

1. Conduct Market Research

Before expanding or scaling a business, it is crucial to conduct comprehensive market research. Identify potential target markets or customer segments that align with your business offerings. Understand their needs, preferences, and buying behavior. Analyze market trends, competition, and potential barriers to entry.

Market research helps you identify growth opportunities and make informed decisions about where and how to expand your business. It allows you to tailor your products or services to meet the specific needs of new markets and position your business effectively against competitors.

2. Develop a Growth Strategy

A growth strategy outlines the roadmap for expanding and scaling your business. It encompasses various elements, such as market entry strategies, product or service expansion plans, marketing and sales strategies, and financial considerations.

Consider the different options available for expansion, such as entering new geographic regions, targeting new customer segments, diversifying product lines, or acquiring complementary businesses. Assess the potential risks, costs, and benefits associated with each strategy. Develop a detailed plan that outlines the necessary resources, timelines, and milestones for achieving growth.

3. Build a Strong Team

Expanding and scaling a business requires a strong team that can handle increased demands and drive growth. Assess your current team's capabilities and identify any gaps. Determine the roles and skill sets needed to support your expansion plans.

Recruit and hire talented individuals who can contribute to your business's growth objectives. Provide ongoing training and development opportunities to ensure your team has the skills and knowledge necessary to excel in their roles. Foster a culture of collaboration, innovation, and continuous improvement to drive success during expansion.

4. Enhance Operational Efficiency

As you scale your business, it becomes essential to enhance operational efficiency to accommodate increased demand. Streamline processes, identify bottlenecks, and implement technology solutions to automate repetitive tasks. Evaluate your supply chain and logistics to ensure timely and cost-effective delivery of products or services.

Invest in scalable infrastructure and systems that can support growth without sacrificing quality or customer satisfaction. Regularly monitor key performance indicators (KPIs) related to production, delivery, and customer service to identify areas for improvement and optimize efficiency.

5. Establish Strategic Partnerships

Strategic partnerships can play a crucial role in expanding your business. Identify potential partners who can provide complementary products, services, or distribution channels. Collaborate with industry influencers, thought leaders, or complementary businesses to leverage their network and reach new customers.

Strategic partnerships can help you enter new markets, expand your customer base, access new resources or technologies, and enhance your brand visibility. However, ensure that partnerships align with your business objectives and maintain mutually beneficial relationships.

6. Leverage Technology and Automation

Technology plays a vital role in scaling a business. Implement software solutions, customer relationship management (CRM) systems, and automation tools to streamline operations, improve productivity, and enhance customer experiences.

For example, invest in an e-commerce platform to facilitate online sales and provide customers with a seamless shopping experience. Implement cloud-based solutions to manage data and resources efficiently. Utilize project management tools to coordinate and track progress on various expansion initiatives.

7. Focus on Marketing and Branding

Expanding a business requires a strategic marketing and branding approach to penetrate new markets and attract new customers. Develop a comprehensive marketing strategy that includes digital marketing, content marketing, social media advertising, public relations, and targeted outreach efforts.

Tailor your marketing messages and tactics to resonate with the specific needs and preferences of your target markets. Build brand awareness and differentiate your business from competitors through effective branding and messaging strategies.

Operations Scaling and Growth Management

As a business expands and experiences growth, it is crucial to effectively manage operations to ensure scalability and maintain quality standards. Operations scaling involves increasing production capacity, optimizing processes, and adapting to meet growing demands. Effective growth management requires strategic planning, resource allocation, and continuous improvement. Here are key considerations for scaling operations and managing growth:

1. Evaluate and Streamline Processes: Assess existing processes and identify areas for improvement. Streamline workflows, eliminate bottlenecks, and optimize efficiency to accommodate increased production demands.

2. Invest in Technology: Adopt technology solutions that support scalability and enhance operational efficiency. Implement enterprise resource planning (ERP) systems, automation tools, and data analytics to streamline operations, improve decision-making, and optimize resource allocation.

3. Build a Scalable Supply Chain: Collaborate with suppliers, distributors, and logistics partners to build a scalable and efficient supply chain. Ensure that your supply chain can handle increased demand, minimize lead times, and maintain product quality.

4. Manage Inventory: Optimize inventory management to avoid stockouts or excess inventory. Implement inventory tracking systems, forecast demand accurately, and establish supplier relationships to support timely deliveries.

5. Develop a Skilled Workforce: Invest in employee training and development to build a skilled and adaptable workforce. Provide opportunities for cross-training and upskilling to meet changing operational needs.

6. Monitor Key Performance Indicators (KPIs): Establish KPIs to track operational performance and identify areas that need improvement. Monitor metrics such as production output, quality standards, customer satisfaction, and fulfillment cycle time.

7. Continuously Improve Processes: Implement a culture of continuous improvement. Encourage employees to provide feedback, identify opportunities for innovation, and suggest process enhancements. Regularly review operations to identify inefficiencies and implement changes for enhanced productivity.

8. Maintain Quality Standards: As operations scale, it is crucial to maintain consistent quality standards. Implement quality control measures, conduct regular audits, and ensure that all employees are aligned with quality objectives.

By effectively managing operations, scaling and growth, businesses can ensure a smooth transition into larger markets, meet increasing customer demands, and maintain operational excellence.

Chapter 6

Overcoming Obstacles and Adversity

Overcoming Obstacles and Adversity

Building a successful business journey is rarely a smooth and straightforward path. Along the way, entrepreneurs often encounter numerous obstacles and face adversity that tests their resilience, determination, and problem-solving skills. Overcoming these challenges is an essential part of the entrepreneurial journey and can ultimately lead to growth and success. In this discussion, we will explore common obstacles and adversities faced by entrepreneurs and strategies for overcoming them.

1. Financial Challenges

One of the most common obstacles entrepreneurs face is financial challenges. Starting a business often requires significant upfront investment, and cash flow can be unpredictable during the early stages. To overcome this obstacle:

a. Develop a detailed financial plan: Create a realistic budget, project cash flow, and identify potential funding sources such as loans, grants, or investors.

b. Seek alternative funding options: Explore crowdfunding platforms, angel investors, or strategic partnerships to secure additional funding.

c. Bootstrap and manage costs: Minimize expenses, negotiate with suppliers, and focus on generating revenue to sustain and grow the business.

2. Market Competition

In today's competitive business landscape, entrepreneurs must navigate intense competition to establish their brand and gain market share. To overcome this obstacle:

a. Conduct thorough market research: Understand your target audience, identify their needs, and differentiate your products or services from competitors.

b. Develop a unique value proposition: Clearly communicate the unique benefits and advantages your business offers compared to competitors.

c. Build strong customer relationships: Focus on exceptional customer service, engage with your audience, and foster loyalty through personalized experiences.

d. Continuously innovate: Stay ahead of the competition by regularly updating your products, exploring new technologies, and adapting to market trends.

3. Limited Resources

Limited resources, such as manpower, technology, or infrastructure, can pose significant challenges for entrepreneurs. To overcome this obstacle:

a. Prioritize tasks and allocate resources efficiently: Identify critical areas that require immediate attention and allocate resources accordingly.

b. Embrace technology and automation: Leverage technology solutions and automation tools to streamline processes and maximize efficiency.

c. Build strategic partnerships: Collaborate with complementary businesses or individuals to access additional resources and expertise.

d. Outsource non-core functions: Consider outsourcing non-core activities to focus on core competencies and conserve resources.

4. Uncertainty and Risk

Entrepreneurship is inherently risky, and uncertainty is a constant companion for business owners. To overcome this obstacle:

a. Embrace a growth mindset: Adopt a positive and adaptable mindset, viewing challenges as opportunities for learning and growth.

b. Develop contingency plans: Anticipate potential risks and develop contingency plans to mitigate their impact.

c. Seek mentorship and advice: Connect with experienced entrepreneurs or industry experts who can provide guidance and insights.

d. Conduct market research and validate ideas: Validate your business ideas and concepts through market research, customer feedback, and testing.

5. Work-Life Balance

Entrepreneurs often face the challenge of balancing work commitments with personal life. Long hours, high levels of stress, and the pressure to succeed can take a toll on well-being. To overcome this obstacle:

a. Set boundaries: Establish clear boundaries between work and personal life, allocating specific time for relaxation, family, and self-care.

b. Delegate and outsource tasks: Delegate responsibilities and outsource tasks to trusted employees or contractors, freeing up time for strategic decision-making.

c. Build a support system: Surround yourself with a supportive network of family, friends, and mentors who can provide guidance and emotional support.

d. Prioritize self-care: Take care of your physical and mental well-being by exercising, practicing mindfulness, and engaging in activities that bring joy and relaxation.

Overcoming Failure and Learning from Mistakes

Failure is an inevitable part of the entrepreneurial journey. It is how entrepreneurs respond to and learn from failure that determines their ultimate success.

Overcoming failure requires resilience, a growth mindset, and the ability to extract valuable lessons from mistakes. Here are key strategies for overcoming failure and learning from mistakes:

1. Embrace a Growth Mindset: Adopt a mindset that sees failure as an opportunity for growth and learning. Understand that setbacks and mistakes are stepping stones on the path to success. Embrace challenges, view them as learning experiences, and believe in your ability to bounce back stronger.

2. Analyze and Reflect: When faced with failure, take the time to analyze what went wrong and reflect on the underlying causes. Identify the factors that led to the failure and evaluate the decisions, strategies, or assumptions that may have contributed to the outcome.

3. Take Responsibility: Accept responsibility for your mistakes and failures. Avoid blaming external factors or others. Taking ownership allows you to learn from the experience and make necessary adjustments moving forward.

4. Learn from Mistakes: Extract valuable lessons from your failures and mistakes. Identify specific actions or decisions that led to the negative outcome and determine how you can improve or avoid similar situations in the future.

5. Seek Feedback and Advice: Reach out to mentors, advisors, or fellow entrepreneurs for feedback and advice. They can provide valuable insights and fresh perspectives on your failures, helping you gain a better understanding of what went wrong and how to improve.

6. Adapt and Pivot: Use the knowledge gained from failure to adapt your strategies and make necessary adjustments. Be willing to pivot, change course, or revise your business plans based on the lessons learned.

7. Persistence and Resilience: Maintain a resilient attitude and persevere in the face of failure. Understand that setbacks are temporary and that success often comes after multiple attempts. Use failure as motivation to keep pushing forward.

8. Celebrate Small Wins: Acknowledge and celebrate small wins along the way. Recognize the progress you've made and the lessons you've learned. This positive reinforcement keeps you motivated and focused on the bigger picture.

9. Continuous Improvement: Develop a culture of continuous improvement within your business. Encourage a learning mindset among your team, where mistakes are seen as opportunities for growth and innovation.

10. Stay Positive: Maintain a positive outlook throughout your entrepreneurial journey. Surround yourself with a support network that uplifts and motivates you during challenging times. A positive mindset can help you bounce back from failure and maintain your enthusiasm and drive.

By embracing failure as a stepping stone to success and actively learning from mistakes, entrepreneurs can grow, adapt, and ultimately achieve their goals. Remember that failure is not the end, but rather an opportunity for growth and future success.

Managing Cash Flow and Financial Difficulty

Cash flow management is a critical aspect of running a successful business. Without effective management, businesses can face financial difficulties that hinder growth and sustainability. Here are key strategies for managing cash flow and overcoming financial challenges:

1. Forecast and Monitor Cash Flow: Develop a detailed cash flow forecast that projects income and expenses over a specific period. Regularly monitor and update the forecast to ensure accuracy and anticipate potential cash flow gaps.

2. Maintain a Cash Reserve: Build a cash reserve to cover unexpected expenses or fluctuations in revenue. Set aside a portion of profits during periods of strong cash flow to create a financial safety net.

3. Control Expenses: Evaluate all expenses and identify areas where costs can be reduced or eliminated. Negotiate with suppliers for favorable terms and discounts, explore cost-saving measures, and prioritize essential expenditures.

4. Improve Receivables Management: Implement effective accounts receivable management practices to ensure timely collection of payments. Set clear payment terms, follow up on overdue invoices, and consider offering incentives for early payments.

5. Optimize Payables: Strategically manage accounts payable to optimize cash flow. Negotiate extended payment terms with suppliers without negatively impacting relationships. Take advantage of early payment discounts where applicable.

6. Explore Financing Options: In times of financial difficulty, consider alternative financing options. Explore small business loans, lines of credit, or invoice financing to bridge temporary cash flow gaps.

7. Strengthen Customer Relationships: Build strong relationships with customers to encourage loyalty and prompt payment. Provide exceptional customer service, address concerns promptly, and establish transparent communication channels.

8. Seek Professional Advice: If facing significant financial challenges, seek advice from financial professionals, accountants, or business advisors. They can provide insights, help create restructuring plans, or suggest alternative financing solutions.

9. Adjust Pricing and Revenue Strategies: Assess pricing strategies to ensure they align with market conditions and profitability goals. Explore opportunities to diversify revenue streams or introduce new products or services to boost cash flow.

10. Regularly Review Financial Performance: Conduct regular financial reviews to assess the overall health of your business. Analyze key financial indicators, identify areas of improvement, and make necessary adjustments to stay on track.

Managing cash flow and overcoming financial difficulties requires proactive planning, diligent monitoring, and strategic decision-making. By implementing these strategies and maintaining financial discipline, businesses can navigate challenges, maintain healthy cash flow, and achieve long-term financial stability.

Chapter 7

Leadership and Team Building

Effective leadership and strong team building are essential components of building a successful business. A skilled leader can inspire, motivate, and guide their team toward achieving shared goals. Moreover, fostering a cohesive and high-performing team is vital for driving innovation, productivity, and overall success. In this section, we will explore key principles and strategies for leadership and team building.

1. Lead by Example:

Effective leaders lead by example, setting the tone and standard for their team. They demonstrate integrity, professionalism, and a strong work ethic. By embodying the values and behaviors they expect from their team members, leaders inspire trust, respect, and commitment.

2. Communicate Openly and Transparently:

Clear and open communication is vital for effective leadership. Leaders should provide regular updates, set clear expectations, and encourage open dialogue. Transparent communication fosters trust, promotes alignment, and ensures everyone is on the same page.

3. Delegate and Empower:

Leaders must delegate tasks and responsibilities to team members, empowering them to make decisions and take ownership of their work. Delegating not only helps distribute the workload but also fosters growth, builds confidence, and enhances team members' skills.

4. Foster a Collaborative Environment:

Encourage collaboration, teamwork, and knowledge sharing among team members. Create a culture that values diversity of ideas and perspectives, promotes active listening, and encourages respectful debate. Collaboration enhances creativity, problem-solving, and overall team performance.

5. Provide Guidance and Support:

Effective leaders provide guidance, support, and mentorship to their team members. They offer constructive feedback, recognize achievements, and provide opportunities for professional growth. Supporting and developing team members not only boosts individual performance but also strengthens the overall team dynamic.

6. Foster a Positive Work Culture:

Create a positive work environment that values employee well-being, work-life balance, and recognition. Encourage a culture of appreciation, celebrate achievements, and promote a sense of belonging and camaraderie. A positive work culture increases employee satisfaction, engagement, and loyalty.

7. Promote Continuous Learning:

Leaders should promote a culture of continuous learning and professional development. Encourage team members to enhance their skills, provide training opportunities, and support their pursuit of personal and career growth. By investing in their development, leaders inspire loyalty and build a high-performing team.

8. Resolve Conflict Effectively:

Conflict is inevitable in any team. Effective leaders address conflicts promptly and constructively. They encourage open dialogue, mediate disputes, and foster a resolution-oriented mindset. Resolving conflicts strengthens relationships, promotes collaboration, and maintains a positive team dynamic.

9. Celebrate Success:

Acknowledge and celebrate team successes and milestones. Recognize individual and collective achievements to boost morale, motivation, and team spirit. Celebrating success fosters a sense of pride, creates a positive work environment, and reinforces a culture of excellence.

10. Continuously Improve Leadership Skills:

Leadership is an ongoing journey of growth and development. Effective leaders are committed to continuously improving their leadership skills. Seek feedback, engage in self-reflection, and invest in leadership training and development to enhance your ability to lead and inspire your team.

Note: Leadership and team building are fundamental to building a successful business. By adopting effective leadership practices, fostering a collaborative team environment, and nurturing individual growth, leaders can create high-performing teams that drive innovation, productivity, and success. Remember that leadership is not just about directing, but also about inspiring and empowering others to achieve their best.

Developing Effective Leadership Capabilities

Effective leadership is a crucial factor in the success of any business. Developing strong leadership capabilities allows individuals to inspire, motivate, and guide their teams towards achieving organizational goals. Effective leaders possess a range of skills and qualities that enable them to navigate challenges, build trust, and drive performance. In this section, we will explore key strategies for developing effective leadership capabilities.

1. Self-Awareness:

Self-awareness is the foundation of effective leadership. It involves understanding one's strengths, weaknesses, values, and impact on others. Engage in self-reflection, seek feedback from others, and continuously strive for personal growth. By understanding yourself, you can lead with authenticity and align your actions with your values.

2. Continuous Learning:

Leadership is an ongoing journey of learning and growth. Stay curious and seek opportunities for continuous learning and development. Read books on leadership, attend workshops and seminars, and engage in networking with other leaders. Embrace new ideas and perspectives to expand your knowledge and enhance your leadership capabilities.

3. Emotional Intelligence:

Emotional intelligence is the ability to recognize, understand, and manage one's own emotions and those of others. Effective leaders leverage emotional intelligence to build strong relationships, inspire trust, and navigate conflicts. Develop empathy, practice active listening, and respond to emotions with empathy and understanding.

4. Effective Communication:

Effective communication is a cornerstone of successful leadership. Hone your communication skills, both verbal and non-verbal, to convey messages clearly and inspire action. Be an active listener, provide feedback, and communicate with transparency and authenticity. Tailor your communication style to different audiences and situations.

5. Building and Leading High-Performing Teams:

Leadership involves building and leading high-performing teams. Develop skills in team building, collaboration, and conflict resolution. Create a positive team culture, set clear expectations, and empower team members to excel. Provide guidance, support, and opportunities for growth to foster a motivated and engaged team.

6. Decision-Making and Problem-Solving:

Leaders must make informed decisions and solve complex problems. Develop critical thinking skills, gather relevant information, analyze options, and consider different perspectives. Practice sound judgment, weigh risks and benefits, and make timely decisions. Learn from failures and setbacks to refine your decision-making abilities.

7. Adaptability and Resilience:

Leadership requires adaptability and resilience in the face of change and challenges. Cultivate a growth mindset, embrace change, and encourage innovation within your team. Be resilient in the face of setbacks, learn from failures, and bounce back stronger. Show flexibility and agility in navigating uncertain and dynamic environments.

8. Relationship Building:

Effective leaders build strong relationships with team members, colleagues, and stakeholders. Invest time in building rapport, understanding individual strengths, and creating connections. Foster a collaborative and inclusive environment where diverse perspectives are valued. Develop trust and credibility through open and transparent communication.

9. Mentorship and Coaching:

Leadership involves mentoring and coaching team members to unlock their full potential. Develop skills in providing constructive feedback, coaching, and mentoring. Support the growth and development of your team members by providing guidance, setting goals, and offering opportunities for learning and advancement.

10. Lead by Example:

Leaders must lead by example and model the behavior they expect from others. Demonstrate integrity, professionalism, and ethical conduct. Show dedication, resilience, and a strong work ethic. By embodying the values and qualities you seek in your team, you inspire trust, respect, and commitment.

Inspiring and Motivating Your Team:
As a leader, one of your primary roles is to inspire and motivate your team to reach new heights of success. The ability to ignite the spark within each team member is a key characteristic of effective leadership. By fostering a culture of inspiration and motivation, you can propel your team towards achieving their goals and driving organizational success. Let's explore some strategies for inspiring and motivating your team to go above and beyond.

1. Lead with Purpose and Passion:

Be a beacon of inspiration by leading with a clear sense of purpose and unwavering passion. Communicate your vision and values, and demonstrate genuine enthusiasm for the work at hand. When your team sees your genuine commitment, it ignites their own passion and motivates them to give their best.

2. Provide Meaningful Feedback and Recognition:

Regularly provide constructive feedback and recognize your team members' achievements. Acknowledge their contributions, highlight their strengths, and provide guidance for improvement. Show appreciation for their efforts and celebrate milestones, both big and small. This recognition fosters a sense of pride, boosts morale, and inspires continued excellence.

3. Encourage Growth and Development:

Invest in the growth and development of your team members. Provide opportunities for learning, skill-building, and career advancement. Support their professional goals and encourage them to take on new challenges. When team members see a clear path for growth, it fuels their motivation and commitment to success.

4. Foster Collaboration and Team Spirit:

Create an environment that values collaboration and teamwork. Encourage open communication, active listening, and respect for diverse perspectives. Foster a sense of camaraderie and shared purpose by organizing team-building activities, encouraging cross-functional collaboration, and promoting a supportive atmosphere. When team members feel connected and supported, it enhances their motivation and productivity.

5. Set Challenging Goals and Celebrate Achievements:

Set ambitious but attainable goals that stretch your team's capabilities. Involve them in the goal-setting process to foster ownership and commitment. Provide the necessary resources and support to help them succeed. Celebrate achievements along the way, recognizing individual and collective accomplishments. This recognition fuels a sense of achievement and inspires continued effort.

6. Lead by Example:

As a leader, your actions speak louder than words. Lead by example and demonstrate the behavior and work ethic you expect from your team. Show integrity, resilience, and a positive attitude even in the face of challenges. When your team sees your commitment and dedication, it inspires them to follow suit.

7. Foster a Positive Work Culture:

Create a positive work culture that values work-life balance, well-being, and mutual respect. Encourage open communication, flexibility, and creativity. Provide opportunities for autonomy and empowerment. A positive work culture fosters a sense of belonging, loyalty, and motivation.

8. Communicate the Impact of Their Work:

Help your team members understand the impact of their work on the organization and its stakeholders. Clearly communicate how their contributions align with the broader goals and mission of the organization. When team members see the value and significance of their work, it inspires a sense of purpose and motivation.

•Inspiring and motivating your team is a powerful leadership skill that drives exceptional performance and fosters a positive work environment. By leading with purpose, providing meaningful feedback, fostering collaboration, setting challenging goals, and creating a supportive culture, you can ignite the spark within each team member. Remember, your role as a leader is not only to manage tasks but to inspire greatness and unleash the full potential of your team.

Value Diversity and Inclusion:

In today's global and interconnected world, valuing diversity and fostering inclusion is not only a moral imperative but also a key driver of organizational success. Embracing diversity means recognizing and appreciating the unique perspectives, backgrounds, and talents that individuals from different cultures, ethnicities, genders, abilities, and identities bring to the table. By creating an inclusive environment where everyone feels valued, respected, and empowered, organizations can tap into the full potential of their diverse workforce. Let's explore the importance of valuing diversity and inclusion.

1. Embracing Different Perspectives:

Diversity brings a wealth of different perspectives and experiences, which can lead to more creative and innovative solutions. When individuals with diverse backgrounds collaborate, they challenge each other's assumptions and contribute unique insights. This diversity of thought fosters creativity and drives the development of new ideas.

2. Fostering Collaboration and Teamwork:

Inclusive environments foster collaboration and teamwork. When team members feel valued and included, they are more likely to contribute their diverse perspectives, share ideas, and collaborate effectively. This collaboration enhances problem-solving, decision-making, and overall team performance.

3. Enhancing Decision-Making:

Diverse teams are better equipped to make well-informed decisions. By considering a range of viewpoints, diverse teams can identify blind spots, minimize biases, and arrive at more comprehensive and balanced decisions. This diversity of perspectives leads to better outcomes and reduces the risk of groupthink.

4. Attracting and Retaining Top Talent:

Organizations that value diversity and inclusion are more attractive to top talent. Inclusivity sends a message that individuals from all backgrounds are welcome and can thrive within the organization. This not only helps attract a diverse pool of candidates but also improves employee retention, as individuals feel a sense of belonging and are more likely to stay with the organization.

5. Enhancing Customer Relations:

Valuing diversity and inclusion is not only important internally but also externally. By embracing diversity, organizations can better understand and serve their diverse customer base. This inclusivity builds trust, enhances customer satisfaction, and improves overall brand reputation.

6. Driving Innovation and Adaptability:

Diverse and inclusive organizations are more adaptable and innovative. By embracing diverse perspectives, organizations can better anticipate and respond to market changes and emerging trends. This adaptability and innovation give organizations a competitive edge in a rapidly evolving business landscape.

Valuing diversity and fostering inclusion is not only the right thing to do but also a strategic imperative for organizations seeking to thrive in a diverse and complex world. By embracing diversity of thought, fostering collaboration, enhancing decision-making, attracting top talent, improving customer relations, and driving innovation, organizations can harness the power of differences and create a culture of inclusion where everyone can contribute their best. Embracing diversity and inclusion is a journey that requires ongoing commitment, education, and a continuous effort to challenge biases and promote equality.

Chapter 8.

Continuous Improvement and Innovation:

In today's rapidly evolving business landscape, organizations must embrace continuous improvement and innovation to stay competitive and thrive. Continuous improvement involves the relentless pursuit of enhancing processes, products, and services, while innovation entails the creation of new and unique solutions that deliver value to customers. By fostering a culture of continuous improvement and encouraging innovation, organizations can drive growth, increase efficiency, and achieve sustainable success. In this discussion, we will explore the importance of continuous improvement and innovation and provide strategies for implementing them effectively.

1. The Importance of Continuous Improvement:

Continuous improvement is a mindset and approach that focuses on incremental and ongoing enhancements to processes, systems, and practices. Here are some key reasons why continuous improvement is crucial for organizational success:

a. Enhancing Efficiency and Productivity: Continuous improvement enables organizations to identify inefficiencies, eliminate waste, and streamline processes. By constantly seeking ways to optimize operations, organizations can enhance efficiency, reduce costs, and improve productivity.

b. Quality Enhancement: Continuous improvement involves a commitment to delivering high-quality products and services. By regularly evaluating and refining processes, organizations can identify and address quality issues, improving customer satisfaction and loyalty.

c. Employee Engagement and Empowerment: Encouraging a culture of continuous improvement empowers employees to contribute their ideas, insights, and suggestions for improvement. Engaged employees who feel their voices are valued are more motivated, innovative, and committed to the organization's success.

d. Adaptation to Change: Continuous improvement fosters an organizational culture that embraces change and adapts to new market dynamics. It enables organizations to stay agile, respond to customer needs, and capitalize on emerging opportunities.

2. Strategies for Continuous Improvement:

To effectively implement continuous improvement, organizations can adopt various strategies:

a. Establish Clear Goals and Metrics: Define specific goals and metrics that align with the organization's vision and objectives. These goals can be related to efficiency, quality, customer satisfaction, or any other area of improvement. Regularly monitor progress and measure performance against these goals.

b. Foster a Learning Culture: Encourage a culture of learning and development where employees are encouraged to seek new knowledge, share ideas, and experiment with new approaches. Provide opportunities for training, mentorship, and cross-functional collaboration to promote continuous learning.

c. Gather and Analyze Data: Collect relevant data and analyze it to gain insights into areas that require improvement. Data-driven decision-making enables organizations to identify trends, patterns, and root causes of problems, guiding their improvement efforts.

d. Promote Collaboration and Communication: Encourage collaboration and open communication channels across teams and departments. Foster a culture where employees feel comfortable sharing their ideas, concerns, and suggestions for improvement. Create platforms for cross-functional collaboration and knowledge sharing.

e. Implement Lean and Agile Methodologies: Embrace lean and agile methodologies, such as Lean Six Sigma or Agile Project Management, to drive continuous improvement. These methodologies provide structured frameworks and tools for identifying bottlenecks, eliminating waste, and optimizing processes.

3. The Significance of Innovation:

Innovation is the process of transforming creative ideas into tangible solutions that address customer needs and create value. It involves taking risks, challenging the status quo, and thinking outside the box. Here are key reasons why innovation is critical for organizational success:

a. Competitive Advantage: Innovation enables organizations to differentiate themselves from competitors. By introducing unique products, services, or business models, organizations can capture market share, attract customers, and gain a competitive edge.

b. Customer-Centricity: Innovation allows organizations to better understand and meet customer needs. By continuously innovating and anticipating customer preferences, organizations can create products and services that deliver superior value and enhance customer satisfaction.

c. Adaptation to Market Trends: Innovation helps organizations stay ahead of market trends and evolving customer demands. It allows organizations to respond to changing market conditions, technological advancements, and disruptive forces. By embracing innovation, organizations can proactively adapt to new realities and seize emerging opportunities.

d. Process Improvement and Efficiency: Innovation goes beyond product or service development. It also encompasses finding innovative ways to improve internal processes, systems, and workflows. By innovating internal operations, organizations can enhance efficiency, reduce costs, and optimize resource utilization.

4. Strategies for Promoting Innovation:

To foster a culture of innovation within an organization, several strategies can be implemented:

a. Encourage Creativity and Risk-Taking: Create an environment where employees feel empowered to generate and share new ideas. Encourage risk-taking and embrace a "fail fast, learn fast" mentality, where mistakes are seen as learning opportunities. Encourage employees to think outside the box and challenge conventional thinking.

b. Promote Cross-Functional Collaboration: Encourage collaboration and knowledge sharing across different departments and teams. Foster a culture of collaboration and open communication that enables diverse perspectives to come together and generate innovative ideas.

c. Provide Resources and Support: Allocate resources, such as time, budget, and technology, to support innovation initiatives. Establish dedicated innovation teams or allocate specific roles for driving innovation within the organization. Provide training, workshops, and resources to enhance employees' innovation capabilities.

d. Embrace Design Thinking and User-Centric Approaches: Adopt design thinking principles to uncover customer needs and develop innovative solutions. Engage with customers through user research, feedback sessions, and co-creation activities. By truly understanding customer pain points and aspirations, organizations can develop products and services that resonate with their target audience.

e. Foster External Partnerships and Collaboration: Seek external partnerships with startups, universities, research institutions, or industry experts to tap into external expertise and insights. Collaborate with external stakeholders to co-create innovative solutions or leverage emerging technologies.

Promote Organizational Innovation:

Innovation is a catalyst for organizational growth and success. It fuels creativity, drives competitive advantage, and propels organizations to stay ahead of the curve. To foster a culture of innovation, organizations must actively promote and support innovation initiatives at all levels. By creating an environment that encourages experimentation, embraces new ideas, and values creativity, organizations can unleash the full potential of their employees and drive transformative change. Let's explore key strategies for promoting organizational innovation.

1. Leadership Support and Vision:

Leadership plays a critical role in promoting innovation within an organization. Leaders must communicate a clear vision for innovation, set the example by embracing new ideas, and provide the necessary resources and support to drive innovation initiatives. When leaders prioritize and actively support innovation, it sends a powerful message to the rest of the organization.

2. Encourage Risk-Taking and Learn from Failure:

Creating a safe space for risk-taking and learning from failure is essential for fostering innovation. Encourage employees to take calculated risks, explore new approaches, and challenge the status quo. Celebrate failures as learning opportunities and encourage employees to share their experiences and lessons learned. Emphasize that failure is an inherent part of the innovation process and that the insights gained from failures can lead to breakthroughs.

3. Promote Collaboration and Cross-Pollination:

Collaboration is a key driver of innovation. Break down silos and encourage cross-functional collaboration to bring diverse perspectives together. Create platforms and spaces for employees to share ideas, exchange knowledge, and collaborate on innovation projects. Foster a culture of open communication and active listening, where everyone's contributions are valued.

4. Provide Resources and Support:

Allocate resources, both financial and human, to support innovation initiatives. Establish dedicated innovation teams or allocate specific roles and responsibilities for driving innovation. Provide training and development opportunities to enhance employees' innovation capabilities. Invest in technology, research, and development to provide the necessary infrastructure for innovation.

5. Encourage Continuous Learning:

Promote a culture of continuous learning and professional development. Encourage employees to acquire new skills, stay updated on emerging trends, and explore innovative practices in their fields. Support employees in attending conferences, workshops, and training programs related to innovation and creativity. Encourage them to share their knowledge and insights with colleagues.

6. Recognize and Reward Innovation:

Recognize and reward employees who contribute to innovation. Celebrate innovative ideas, successful projects, and creative problem-solving. Create formal recognition programs that highlight and appreciate employees' innovative contributions. This recognition reinforces the importance of innovation within the organization and motivates others to actively participate in the innovation process.

7. Foster an Entrepreneurial Mindset:

Encourage employees to think like entrepreneurs and take ownership of their ideas and projects. Empower them to be proactive, embrace autonomy, and pursue innovative solutions. Create an environment that values entrepreneurial thinking, where employees are encouraged to identify and seize opportunities.

Keep an Eye on Industry Trends and Competitors:

In today's fast-paced and competitive business landscape, it is crucial for organizations to keep a close watch on industry trends and competitors. Staying informed about the latest developments, emerging technologies, and shifts in customer preferences allows organizations to anticipate changes, identify opportunities, and proactively adapt their strategies. By monitoring industry trends and competitors, organizations can stay ahead of the curve and maintain a competitive edge. Let's explore the importance of keeping an eye on industry trends and competitors.

1. Anticipating Market Shifts:

Monitoring industry trends helps organizations anticipate market shifts and changes in customer demands. By staying informed about emerging technologies, evolving consumer preferences, and disruptive innovations, organizations can align their strategies and offerings to meet future needs. Anticipating market shifts allows organizations to be proactive rather than reactive, positioning themselves for success in changing market dynamics.

2. Identifying Competitive Advantages:

Keeping a close watch on competitors enables organizations to identify their strengths, weaknesses, and unique value propositions. By studying their strategies, product offerings, and customer experiences, organizations can gain insights into areas where they can differentiate themselves and create a competitive advantage. This knowledge helps organizations refine their own value proposition and make informed decisions about product development, pricing, and marketing strategies.

3. Innovation and Continuous Improvement:

Monitoring industry trends and competitors fosters a culture of innovation and continuous improvement within organizations. By observing the latest innovations and best practices in the industry, organizations can identify areas for improvement and implement innovative solutions. This knowledge inspires creativity, sparks new ideas, and encourages organizations to push the boundaries of what is possible.

4. Customer-Centricity:

Industry trends and competitor analysis provide valuable insights into customer preferences, needs, and expectations. By understanding customer behavior and staying attuned to changing trends, organizations can tailor their products, services, and marketing efforts to better serve their target audience. This customer-centric approach enhances customer satisfaction, loyalty, and retention.

5. Opportunities for Collaboration and Partnerships:

Monitoring industry trends and competitors also presents opportunities for collaboration and partnerships. Organizations can identify potential synergies with complementary businesses, explore joint ventures, or engage in strategic alliances to leverage each other's strengths and create mutually beneficial opportunities. Collaborating with industry players can enhance innovation, expand market reach, and create new revenue streams.

6. Agility and Adaptability:

Keeping an eye on industry trends and competitors allows organizations to be agile and adaptable. By staying informed about the changing landscape, organizations can respond quickly to market shifts, adjust their strategies, and seize emerging opportunities. This agility enables organizations to stay ahead of the competition and navigate uncertainties more effectively.

Creating a Continuous Improvement Culture:

A continuous improvement culture is a mindset and set of practices that foster an environment of ongoing learning, innovation, and growth within an organization. It involves engaging employees at all levels to identify areas for improvement, generate ideas, and drive incremental changes that lead to overall organizational excellence. By creating a culture that values continuous improvement, organizations can enhance efficiency, drive innovation, and stay ahead in a rapidly changing business landscape. Let's explore the key elements of creating a continuous improvement culture.

1. Leadership Commitment:

Leadership commitment is crucial for creating a continuous improvement culture. Leaders must champion the importance of continuous improvement, communicate its value, and lead by example. When leaders actively engage in continuous improvement initiatives, it sends a powerful message to the rest of the organization and reinforces the culture of improvement.

2. Employee Empowerment:

Empowering employees to actively participate in the continuous improvement process is essential. Encourage employees to contribute their ideas, share their insights, and take ownership of improvement initiatives. Create channels and platforms for employees to voice their suggestions and concerns. Recognize and reward employees for their contributions, fostering a sense of ownership and motivation.

3. Open Communication and Collaboration:

Promote open communication and collaboration across all levels of the organization. Encourage employees to share their ideas, perspectives, and feedback freely. Foster a safe and supportive environment where everyone's contributions are valued. Facilitate cross-functional collaboration to encourage diverse viewpoints and harness collective intelligence for problem-solving and process improvement.

4. Continuous Learning and Development:

Nurture a culture of continuous learning and development. Provide training opportunities to enhance employees' skills and knowledge. Encourage employees to seek out new information, stay updated on industry trends, and explore innovative practices. Foster a learning environment where mistakes are seen as learning opportunities and experimentation is encouraged.

5. Establishing Metrics and Feedback Loops:

Establish metrics and feedback mechanisms to measure and track progress in continuous improvement efforts. Define key performance indicators (KPIs) that align with organizational goals and objectives. Regularly review and analyze performance data to identify areas for improvement. Provide constructive feedback to employees, recognizing their contributions and offering guidance for improvement.

6. Process Standardization and Documentation:

Standardize processes and document best practices to ensure consistency and enable continuous improvement. Clearly define standard operating procedures (SOPs) to establish a baseline for improvement. Continuously review and update processes to eliminate waste, enhance efficiency, and streamline operations.

7. Celebrating Achievements:

Recognize and celebrate achievements in continuous improvement. Acknowledge and appreciate individuals and teams for their contributions to the organization's improvement journey. Celebrate milestones and successes, reinforcing the value and importance of continuous improvement efforts.

8. Encouraging Innovation:

While continuous improvement focuses on incremental changes, it's essential to foster a culture of innovation within the organization. Encourage employees to think creatively, challenge conventional thinking, and generate breakthrough ideas. Provide resources and support for innovative projects, enabling employees to explore new opportunities for improvement and growth.

Chapter 9:

Scaling to CEO: How to Take Your Company to the Next Level

Scaling a company to the next level is a significant milestone for any entrepreneur. As the founder, your role evolves from being a hands-on operator to a visionary leader who sets the strategic direction for the organization. The transition to becoming a CEO requires a shift in mindset, new skills, and effective strategies for managing growth. In this guide, we will explore key considerations and actionable steps to help you navigate the journey of scaling your company and assuming the role of CEO.

1. Clarify Your Vision and Strategy:

As you scale your company, it is essential to have a clear vision and strategy for the future. Revisit your mission, values, and long-term goals. Define your market position, target audience, and unique value proposition. Develop a comprehensive strategy that aligns with your vision and sets the direction for growth.

2. Build a Strong Leadership Team:

As CEO, you need to surround yourself with a capable and dedicated leadership team. Identify individuals who complement your skills and bring diverse expertise to the table. Delegate responsibilities and empower your team to drive results. Foster a culture of collaboration, trust, and accountability within your leadership team.

3. Develop Effective Communication Skills:

Effective communication is vital as a CEO. Enhance your communication skills to articulate your vision, goals, and expectations clearly. Foster open and transparent communication with your team, stakeholders, and investors. Ensure everyone understands the company's direction and their role in achieving its objectives.

4. Establish Systems and Processes:

Scaling a company requires efficient systems and processes. Evaluate your existing operations and identify areas that need improvement. Implement scalable systems that can handle increased volumes and maintain quality. Streamline workflows, automate repetitive tasks, and establish clear procedures to ensure consistency and efficiency as the company grows.

5. Manage Financials and Resources:

As CEO, you need a deep understanding of your company's financials and resource management. Monitor cash flow, revenue streams, and expenses closely. Develop financial projections and budgeting strategies to support growth. Secure additional funding or investment if needed to fuel expansion plans.

6. Focus on Talent Acquisition and Retention:

Attracting and retaining top talent is crucial for scaling your company successfully. Develop a strong employer brand that attracts skilled professionals. Implement a comprehensive recruitment process and invest in employee development and engagement initiatives. Create a positive work culture that fosters growth, recognizes achievements, and offers competitive compensation packages.

7. Foster Innovation and Adaptability:

To stay competitive and continue growing, foster a culture of innovation and adaptability within your organization. Encourage creative thinking, experimentation, and continuous learning. Stay abreast of market trends, emerging technologies, and customer needs. Embrace change and be willing to adapt your strategies and offerings as required.

8. Establish Strategic Partnerships:

Strategic partnerships can accelerate your company's growth and open new opportunities. Identify potential partners that align with your vision and can offer complementary products, services, or expertise. Collaborate with industry leaders, investors, suppliers, or distributors to expand your reach and access new markets.

9. Prioritize Customer Satisfaction:

Maintain a relentless focus on customer satisfaction and retention. Listen to customer feedback, identify pain points, and continuously improve your products or services based on their needs. Build strong customer relationships and provide exceptional support to nurture long-term loyalty.

10. Seek Mentorship and Continuous Learning:

As you navigate the journey of scaling your company and assuming the role of CEO, seek mentorship from experienced entrepreneurs or industry experts. Surround yourself with a network of advisors who can provide guidance and support. Invest in your personal and professional development through ongoing learning, workshops, and industry conferences.

Taking on the Role of CEO:
Assuming the role of CEO is a significant milestone in an entrepreneur's journey. It marks the transition from being a founder or manager to becoming the leader responsible for driving the company's overall success. As CEO, you carry the weight of leadership and have the opportunity to shape the direction of the organization. Let's explore the key aspects of taking on the role of CEO.

1. Visionary Leadership:

As CEO, you must provide a clear and compelling vision for the company. Define the purpose and long-term goals that inspire and motivate your team. Communicate this vision consistently, ensuring everyone understands and aligns with the direction in which the organization is heading.

2. Strategic Decision-Making:

CEOs are responsible for making strategic decisions that shape the company's future. Analyze market trends, assess risks, and evaluate growth opportunities. Make informed decisions that drive the organization forward and deliver sustainable results. Consider input from your leadership team and seek advice from trusted advisors when needed.

3. Building and Leading a High-Performing Team:

One of the crucial aspects of being a CEO is building and leading a high-performing team. Surround yourself with talented individuals who share your vision and complement your skills. Nurture a culture of collaboration, trust, and accountability. Provide guidance, support, and mentorship to help your team members grow and excel.

4. Stakeholder Management:

CEOs must effectively manage relationships with stakeholders, including employees, investors, customers, suppliers, and the community. Develop strong relationships based on trust, transparency, and open communication. Address concerns, seek feedback, and ensure the needs and expectations of stakeholders are met.

5. Continuous Learning and Personal Development:

Taking on the role of CEO requires ongoing learning and personal development. Stay informed about industry trends, emerging technologies, and best practices. Seek opportunities to expand your knowledge and skills through executive education, networking events, and mentorship programs. Continuously develop your leadership capabilities to adapt to the evolving business landscape.

6. Balancing Short-Term Results with Long-Term Vision:

CEOs need to strike a balance between achieving short-term results and maintaining a long-term vision. Focus on immediate priorities while keeping the broader strategic goals in mind. Make decisions that balance immediate needs with sustainable growth and profitability.

7. Embracing Responsibility and Accountability:

CEOs are ultimately responsible for the overall performance and success of the organization. Embrace this responsibility and hold yourself accountable for the outcomes. Take ownership of both successes and failures, learn from mistakes, and make necessary adjustments to drive continuous improvement.

8. Effective Communication:

Communication is a critical skill for CEOs. Articulate your vision, expectations, and strategy clearly and consistently. Engage in active listening, encourage open dialogue, and provide regular updates to keep stakeholders informed. Communication builds trust, alignment, and a sense of purpose within the organization.

Strategic Thinking and Strategic Planning:

In today's complex and dynamic business landscape, strategic thinking and strategic planning are vital for organizations to achieve their goals and stay competitive. Strategic thinking involves the ability to envision the future, identify opportunities, and make informed decisions that align with the organization's long-term objectives. Strategic planning is the process of translating strategic thinking into a comprehensive roadmap that guides the allocation of resources and actions needed to achieve those objectives. Let's explore the key concepts and benefits of strategic thinking and strategic planning.

Strategic Thinking:

Strategic thinking is a mindset that focuses on the big picture and long-term goals of an organization. It goes beyond day-to-day operations and encourages leaders to analyze trends, anticipate changes, and envision the future. Here are key elements of strategic thinking:

1. Visionary Perspective: Strategic thinking requires leaders to have a clear vision of where the organization is heading and how it will create value in the future. This involves considering market trends, customer needs, and emerging technologies to identify opportunities and define the organization's strategic direction.

2. External Environment Analysis: Strategic thinkers continuously monitor and analyze the external environment, including industry trends, competitors, and regulatory changes. This allows them to identify threats and opportunities and adjust their strategies accordingly.

3. Internal Assessment: Strategic thinking involves evaluating the organization's strengths, weaknesses, capabilities, and resources. This helps leaders identify areas of competitive advantage and determine how to leverage them effectively.

4. Long-Term Perspective: Strategic thinking takes into account the long-term impact of decisions and actions. It focuses on sustainable growth and considers the organization's position in the market over time.

Strategic Planning:

Strategic planning is the process of translating strategic thinking into actionable plans and initiatives. It provides a structured framework for allocating resources, setting goals, and implementing strategies to achieve the organization's objectives. Here are key components of strategic planning:

1. Goal Setting: Strategic planning involves defining clear and measurable goals that align with the organization's vision and mission. These goals should be specific, achievable, and relevant to the organization's long-term success.

2. Environmental Analysis: Strategic planning includes a comprehensive analysis of the external and internal factors that impact the organization. This analysis helps identify opportunities and threats and informs the development of strategies.

3. Strategy Development: Strategic planning involves formulating strategies to achieve the defined goals. This includes identifying target markets, developing value propositions, and determining competitive positioning.

4. Resource Allocation: Strategic planning involves allocating resources, including financial, human, and technological resources, to support the execution of strategies. It ensures that resources are deployed effectively to achieve the desired outcomes.

5. Implementation and Execution: Strategic planning includes developing action plans, assigning responsibilities, and monitoring progress towards the goals. It involves setting milestones, tracking key performance indicators (KPIs), and making adjustments as needed.

6. Evaluation and Review: Strategic planning requires periodic evaluation and review of the strategies and their outcomes. This helps leaders assess the effectiveness of the plans, identify areas for improvement, and make necessary adjustments to stay on track.

Benefits of Strategic Thinking and Strategic Planning:
Strategic thinking and strategic planning offer several benefits to organizations:

1. Alignment: Strategic thinking and planning align the organization's efforts with its long-term goals, ensuring that everyone is working towards a common vision.

2. Competitive Advantage: Strategic thinking allows organizations to identify unique opportunities and develop strategies that provide a competitive edge in the market.

3. Adaptability: Strategic planning enables organizations to anticipate and respond to changes in the business environment effectively. It helps them stay agile and make proactive adjustments to maintain a competitive position.

4. Resource Optimization: Strategic planning ensures that resources are allocated efficiently and effectively, maximizing their impact on achieving organizational goals.

5. Risk Management: Strategic thinking and planning involve assessing risks and developing contingency plans to mitigate potential challenges. This allows organizations to be better prepared and respond to unexpected events.

6. Innovation and Growth: Strategic thinking fosters a culture of innovation by encouraging leaders to explore new ideas and approaches. Strategic planning provides a framework to implement innovative strategies that drive growth and expansion.

7. Decision-Making: Strategic thinking enhances decision-making by considering long-term implications and weighing various alternatives. It allows leaders to make informed decisions that align with the organization's overall strategy.

8. Alignment of Resources: Strategic planning ensures that resources, such as finances, manpower, and technology, are allocated in a way that supports the organization's strategic objectives. It avoids misallocation and maximizes the utilization of resources.

9. Communication and Alignment: Strategic planning facilitates communication and alignment among different stakeholders within the organization. It helps everyone understand the organization's direction and their role in achieving the strategic goals.

10. Measurable Progress: Strategic planning sets clear goals and KPIs, enabling organizations to track their progress. It provides a framework for evaluating performance and making data-driven decisions to drive continuous improvement.

Establishing Strategic Alliances and Partnerships:

In today's interconnected business landscape, organizations are increasingly turning to strategic alliances and partnerships to drive growth, expand market reach, and enhance competitiveness. Strategic alliances and partnerships involve collaboration between organizations to leverage their respective strengths, resources, and expertise. By establishing strategic alliances and partnerships, organizations can access new markets, share risks, pool resources, and foster innovation. Let's explore the key benefits and considerations in establishing strategic alliances and partnerships.

Benefits of Strategic Alliances and Partnerships:

1. Access to New Markets and Customers: Strategic alliances and partnerships enable organizations to access new markets, customer segments, and distribution channels. By partnering with established players in target markets, organizations can leverage their partner's network and customer base to expand their reach more efficiently.

2. Resource Sharing and Cost Reduction: Strategic alliances and partnerships allow organizations to share resources, including technology, expertise, and infrastructure. This sharing of resources reduces costs, accelerates product development, and enhances operational efficiency.

3. Risk Mitigation: Collaborating with strategic partners helps organizations share risks associated with market entry, product development, or expansion. By spreading risks across multiple parties, organizations can minimize their exposure and increase their chances of success.

4. Innovation and Knowledge Exchange: Strategic alliances and partnerships foster innovation and knowledge exchange. Organizations can tap into their partner's expertise, insights, and best practices to drive innovation, develop new products, or improve existing offerings. This collaboration often leads to creative problem-solving and the generation of new ideas.

5. Competitive Advantage: By forming strategic alliances and partnerships, organizations can gain a competitive advantage. Collaborating with industry leaders or complementary businesses allows organizations to leverage their

partner's strengths and capabilities, creating synergies that enhance their overall competitiveness.

Considerations in Establishing Strategic Alliances and Partnerships:

1. Shared Goals and Vision: It is essential to ensure that potential partners share similar goals, values, and vision. Alignment in strategic objectives increases the likelihood of a successful collaboration and minimizes conflicts in the future.

2. Complementary Strengths and Resources: Organizations should seek partners with complementary strengths and resources. This synergy allows both parties to leverage their unique capabilities and create a mutually beneficial relationship.

3. Trust and Communication: Establishing trust and maintaining open communication is crucial in strategic alliances and partnerships. Transparency, regular updates, and effective communication channels foster collaboration and ensure that both parties are aligned on objectives and expectations.

4. Clear Roles and Responsibilities: Clearly defining roles, responsibilities, and decision-making processes is vital in strategic alliances and partnerships. Establishing governance structures and agreements that outline the rights and obligations of each party promotes clarity and minimizes misunderstandings.

5. Flexibility and Adaptability: Collaboration requires flexibility and adaptability. Organizations should be willing to adapt to changing circumstances, market dynamics, or partner needs. Flexibility allows for the exploration of new opportunities and the adjustment of strategies as required.

Striking a Balance Between Growth and Sustainability:

In the pursuit of organizational success, it is essential to strike a delicate balance between growth and sustainability. While growth fuels expansion and profitability, sustainability ensures long-term viability and responsible business practices. Finding the equilibrium between these two aspects is critical for building a thriving future.

Growth is often associated with increasing market share, revenue, and customer base. However, growth without sustainability can lead to negative consequences such as overconsumption of resources, environmental degradation, and social inequities. On the other hand, a sole focus on sustainability may hinder growth potential and competitiveness.

Organizations must adopt a holistic approach that integrates growth with sustainability. This involves:

1. Responsible Resource Management: Embrace sustainable practices in resource utilization, energy efficiency, waste reduction, and responsible sourcing. Optimize processes to minimize environmental impact while driving growth.

2. Ethical Business Practices: Uphold ethical standards in all aspects of operations, including fair labor practices, diversity and inclusion, and community engagement. Build trust among stakeholders through transparent and responsible business practices.

3. Innovation and Adaptability: Foster a culture of innovation to develop sustainable products and services that meet evolving customer needs. Embrace emerging technologies and market trends to drive growth while minimizing environmental and social impact.

4. Stakeholder Engagement: Engage with stakeholders, including employees, customers, communities, and investors, to understand their expectations and incorporate their perspectives into decision-making. Consider the interests of all stakeholders to achieve a balanced approach.

5. Long-Term Perspective: Take a long-term view of success, considering the impact of decisions and actions on future generations. Balance short-term gains with long-term sustainability, ensuring the organization's growth is built on a solid foundation.

By striking a balance between growth and sustainability, organizations can thrive in the present while ensuring a sustainable future. It requires a commitment to responsible business practices, innovative thinking, and engagement with stakeholders. With a holistic approach, organizations can achieve both growth and sustainability, creating a positive impact on the environment, society, and their own long-term success.

Chapter 10:

Final Thoughts on the Epic Journey to CEO.

Becoming a CEO is the culmination of a remarkable and often challenging journey for any entrepreneur. From humble beginnings to scaling a business, the path to CEO is marked by perseverance, resilience, and a relentless pursuit of success. As we conclude this guide, let's reflect on the key lessons and final thoughts on the epic journey to CEO.

1. Embrace the Journey:
The journey to CEO is not solely about reaching the destination; it is about embracing the entire journey. Embrace the challenges, setbacks, and triumphs along the way. Each experience offers valuable lessons and opportunities for growth. Embracing the journey allows you to learn, adapt, and develop the skills necessary to succeed as a CEO.

2. Continuous Learning and Growth:
As a CEO, the learning journey never ends. Commit to continuous learning and personal growth. Stay curious, seek new knowledge, and embrace opportunities to expand your skill set. Invest in your professional development and surround yourself with mentors and advisors who can provide guidance and support.

3. Lead with Integrity and Purpose:
Leadership is not just about making decisions; it's about leading with integrity, purpose, and authenticity. Define your values and lead by example. Demonstrate ethical behavior, transparency, and a genuine commitment to your organization's mission and values. Inspire and motivate your team to align their efforts with a shared purpose.

4. Foster a Culture of Innovation:
As a CEO, fostering a culture of innovation is vital for organizational success. Encourage creative thinking, celebrate risk-taking, and create an environment

where new ideas are welcomed and embraced. Foster collaboration, empower your team, and provide the necessary resources and support to drive innovation.

5. Surround Yourself with the Right Team:

Success as a CEO relies on building a strong and capable team. Surround yourself with talented individuals who complement your skills and share your vision. Nurture a culture of collaboration, trust, and accountability. Empower your team members and provide opportunities for growth and development.

6. Embrace Change and Adaptability:

In today's rapidly evolving business landscape, change is inevitable. Embrace change and be adaptable. Stay attuned to market trends, emerging technologies, and customer needs. Adapt your strategies and approaches as necessary to stay ahead of the curve.

7. Prioritize Work-Life Balance:

While the journey to CEO can be demanding, it's crucial to prioritize work-life balance. Take care of your physical and mental well-being. Find time for personal interests, hobbies, and quality time with loved ones. Balancing your professional and personal life will help you sustain long-term success and fulfillment.

8. Make a Positive Impact:

As a CEO, you have the opportunity to make a positive impact not only within your organization but also in the wider community. Consider the social and environmental implications of your decisions. Incorporate sustainable practices, support social causes, and contribute to the betterment of society.

9. Celebrate Milestones and Successes:

Throughout your journey to CEO, take time to celebrate milestones and successes. Acknowledge the achievements of your team and express gratitude for their contributions. Celebrating milestones builds a positive and supportive culture, fostering motivation and a sense of pride.

10. Never Stop Dreaming:

Finally, as a CEO, never stop dreaming and setting new goals. The journey does not end at the CEO title; it is merely a stepping stone to new possibilities. Keep pushing boundaries, challenging yourself, and dreaming big. Your determination and passion will continue to drive your success.

Rejoicing in Successes and Milestones:
Throughout the journey to CEO, it is important to take moments to rejoice in the successes and milestones achieved along the way. Celebrating these achievements not only acknowledges the hard work and dedication that went into reaching them but also serves as a source of motivation and inspiration for the future. Here are some reasons why rejoicing in successes and milestones is crucial:

1. Acknowledgment of Progress: Celebrating successes and milestones allows you to pause and reflect on how far you have come. It provides an opportunity to appreciate the progress made and the milestones achieved, which can boost confidence and reaffirm your commitment to the journey.

2. Motivation and Inspiration: Rejoicing in successes and milestones serves as a powerful motivator. It energizes you and your team, reminding you of the positive outcomes that can be achieved through hard work and perseverance. It inspires you to keep pushing forward, even when faced with challenges.

3. Reinforcement of a Positive Culture: Celebrating successes and milestones creates a positive and supportive culture within the organization. It encourages a sense of camaraderie, collaboration, and appreciation among team members. This positive culture enhances morale, fosters a sense of pride, and strengthens the bond within the team.

4. Recognition of Efforts: Celebrating successes and milestones is an opportunity to recognize and appreciate the efforts and contributions of individuals and teams. It provides a platform to acknowledge their hard work, dedication, and achievements. This recognition not only boosts morale but also encourages a sense of ownership and motivation among team members.

5. Milestone Markers for Reflection: Celebrating milestones provides an opportunity for reflection and evaluation. It allows you to assess the journey, identify lessons learned, and make adjustments for future growth. It serves as a reminder of the progress made and the lessons gained, helping to inform future strategies and decisions.

Lessons Learned and Future Entrepreneurial Advice:
The journey to becoming a successful entrepreneur and CEO is filled with valuable lessons and experiences that shape both personal and professional growth. Reflecting on these lessons and using them as a foundation for future endeavors is crucial for continued success. Here are some key lessons learned and future entrepreneurial advice to consider:

1. Embrace Failure as a Stepping Stone: Failure is inevitable on the path to success. Embrace failure as an opportunity to learn, grow, and refine your approach. Use setbacks as stepping stones to drive innovation and make necessary adjustments.

2. Surround Yourself with a Strong Support Network: Building a strong support network is essential. Surround yourself with mentors, advisors, and like-minded individuals who can provide guidance, support, and valuable insights. Collaborate with people who believe in your vision and can offer different perspectives.

3. Adaptability in the Face of Change: The business landscape is constantly evolving. Cultivate adaptability to navigate changing market trends, technologies, and customer preferences. Embrace new opportunities, be open to change, and continuously assess and adjust your strategies.

4. Focus on Building Relationships: Relationships are key to success in entrepreneurship. Invest time in building meaningful connections with customers, suppliers, employees, and stakeholders. Nurture these relationships through open communication, trust, and delivering on commitments.

5. Continuous Learning and Personal Growth: Never stop learning and growing as an entrepreneur. Seek out opportunities for personal and professional development,

whether through workshops, industry conferences, or networking events. Stay curious and stay informed about emerging trends and best practices.

6. Prioritize Work-Life Balance: Entrepreneurship can be all-consuming, but it's important to maintain a healthy work-life balance. Take time for self-care, personal relationships, and hobbies that bring you joy. Balancing work and personal life enhances overall well-being and prevents burnout.

7. Remain Customer-Centric: Always prioritize the needs and preferences of your customers. Continuously gather feedback, listen to their voices, and adapt your products or services to meet their evolving demands. Customer satisfaction is the foundation of a successful business.

8. Take Calculated Risks: Entrepreneurship inherently involves taking risks. However, it's important to take calculated risks by conducting thorough research, analyzing data, and assessing potential outcomes. Mitigate risks by having contingency plans and understanding the potential rewards.

9. Foster a Culture of Innovation: Encourage a culture of innovation within your organization. Empower your team to think creatively, share ideas, and challenge the status quo. Provide resources and support for experimentation and continuous improvement.

10. Stay Passionate and Persistent: Passion and persistence are key drivers of entrepreneurial success. Stay passionate about your vision and remain persistent in the face of challenges. Believe in yourself and your abilities, and don't be deterred by setbacks.

The End of One Adventure and the Start of Another:
As the journey to CEO comes to an end, it marks not only a significant milestone but also the beginning of a new adventure. The transition from entrepreneur to CEO signifies the evolution of your role and responsibilities, and it opens doors to new opportunities and challenges. Here's a reflection on the end of one adventure and the start of another:

1. Reflection and Appreciation: Take a moment to reflect on the achievements, lessons, and growth that have come with the entrepreneurial journey. Appreciate the hard work, dedication, and resilience that have brought you to this point. Celebrate the successes, milestones, and personal milestones achieved along the way.

2. Embrace the CEO Role: Embracing the CEO role means stepping into a position of leadership and responsibility. As CEO, you have the power to shape the future of your organization, inspire your team, and make a positive impact. Embrace the new challenges, opportunities, and responsibilities that come with this role.

3. Continuous Learning and Development: Recognize that the journey to CEO is a continuous learning process. Strive for personal and professional development, seeking opportunities to expand your knowledge, skills, and leadership capabilities. Invest in executive education, mentorship, and networking to support your growth as a CEO.

4. Build on Past Successes: Use the accomplishments and lessons from your entrepreneurial journey as a foundation for future success. Apply the skills, knowledge, and insights gained to make informed decisions, drive innovation, and set strategic goals that align with your organization's vision.

5. Embrace New Adventures: Embrace the uncertainty and excitement that comes with embarking on a new adventure as CEO. Embrace the challenges and setbacks as opportunities for growth and improvement. Stay open to new ideas, trends, and technologies that can shape the future of your organization.

6. Lead with Purpose and Impact: As you embark on this new adventure, lead with purpose and a clear sense of the impact you want to make. Align your business strategies with your values and the needs of your stakeholders. Create a positive organizational culture that inspires your team and attracts top talent.

7. Embrace Change and Adaptability: The journey as CEO will involve navigating through change and uncertainty. Embrace change, adapt to new market dynamics,

and anticipate future trends. Foster a culture of adaptability and innovation within your organization to stay ahead in a rapidly evolving business landscape.

8. Enjoy the Journey: Remember to enjoy the journey. While the responsibilities and challenges of the CEO role may be demanding, cherish the moments of growth, collaboration, and success. Celebrate milestones, foster positive relationships, and find joy in the impact you create through your leadership.

Conclusion:

In conclusion, "From Zero to CEO: The Epic Journey of Building a Successful Business," we have explored the transformative journey of entrepreneurs on their path to becoming successful CEOs. This book highlights the importance of strategic thinking, leadership, innovation, and perseverance in building a thriving business. It emphasizes the value of celebrating milestones, embracing failures as opportunities for growth, and balancing growth with sustainability. As you embark on your own journey, remember to nurture your vision, foster innovation, build meaningful relationships, and make a positive impact. Success is not just about reaching the destination but about embracing the entire journey with determination and passion. May this book inspire and empower you on your epic journey from zero to CEO.

www.ingramcontent.com/pod-product-compliance
Lightning Source LLC
Chambersburg PA
CBHW080933260726
48661CB00010B/3899